THE HISTORY of SHEPPEY

by
LISA TYLER

Published by
B.A. Fitch, 48 High St, Sheerness, Kent, ME12 1NL   Tel: 0795 660273

To the reader

This history of Sheppey has been written at the request of many friends who desire to know something of Sheppey's past

Originally, the work was written as a series of separate articles, therefore some repitition may be found, but I hope the reader will pardon this and enjoy the book as a narrative rather than a text-book of Sheppey history.

I wish to thank all my friends who have helped me by lending material relating to Sheppey and for their advice in correcting this book

A special thanks to Barbara Greenstreet, Bob Fountain, Andy Brown and Minster Gatehouse who have all contributed time and energies to make this book possible.

Lisa Tyler

LISA TYLER

Lisa has had articles published in Bye-Gone Kent, Kent Life and local newspapers

She has prepared the travel guide for the Graham Cumming Group and has also contributed to the Shell Book on Islands of Great Britain.

Lisa provided all the information on Sheppey for the television producer and crew when they filmed Sheppey in 'Country Ways'

She has also lectured on local history at Minster College (Adult Education Department) for two years, and was appointed by Kent University to present a series of lectures on local history at the Teachers Training Centre, Borden.

Lisa has broadcast several times on BBC Radio Kent and recorded on television as the 'Voice of Sheppey' in the shape of the nation and was a member of the North East Kent Writers Circle.

The Publishers

Printed and bound in Great Britain by
Biddles Ltd, Guildford and King's Lynn

CONTENTS

Hasted's late eighteenth century map of Sheppey when Sheerness was hardly as big as Minster.

1 A SHORT GENERAL HISTORY OF SHEPPEY

The history of Sheppey is full of exciting episodes and far reaching influences. Although detatched from the Mainland it has shared the fortunes of the County of Kent which has been invaded by land, sea and air, but the emblem of the White Horse of Kent bears the proud inscription 'Invicta'.

Sheppey is first mentioned in "Geographike Huphegesis" written by the Grecian historian, Ptolemy in the year 161 A.D. It was then called "Toliapis" and regarded as one of the gates to the River Thames. Situated as it is at the mouth of the Medway and separated from the mainland by the Swale, it was a strategic point of defence when invaders sailed through the Swale en route for London.

The Island is about 9 miles long and 4 miles wide and contains some 22,400 acres. The southern side is marshland, and on the northern side, overlooking the estuary of the Thames, the ground rises to the cliffs which consist of London clay and have suffered from erosion for centuries. Many hundreds of acres of land have been lost in this way.

Millions of years ago Sheppey was formed by the delta of an ancient river and rich alluvial soil was washed down into the delta. In this London clay are to be found rich deposits of fossil tropical vegetation dating from ten to twenty million years ago, including the remains of 220 distinct kinds of fishes, birds and insects, the greater number of which are species now extinct.

This London clay has furnished practically all the information regarding the birds which inhabited England during the early period. Six species of sharks, seven species of turtle and terrapins and over a hundred species of vegetables life including Nippa Palm, Eucalyptus, nuts and berries and other tropical plants have also been discovered in Sheppey.

Evidence of early man has been proved by the discovery in 1879 of a complete Bronze Age foundry (now in Ashmolean Museum) an ancient Saxon earthworks at Harty, a tumulus near Borstall Hall and three earthworks at Queenborough. Sheppey was known to the Romans, who named it Insula Ovinium, (The Isle of Sheep). There is no great evidence of extensive Roman occupation on the island, but it is probable that there was a Specula or look out post established at Minster, and that it was garrisioned from Faversham by way of Harty Ferry.

A few Roman remains have been discovered, a kiln was found in 1874 near Shellness Point, a few tiles, a piece of Samian ware and coins of Constantine, a quern at Harty, a gold coin of Saverus in the cliffs, a gold stater at Minster and other coins near the Abbey and Roman tiles can be seen in Sexburga's chapel in Minster church; a small vase; a Roman key and a heart box were discovered at Warden. No other signs of occupation have so far been found. This would seem to confirm the theory that the Roman occupation of Sheppey was one of expediency.

The Romans dominated Britain for five hundred years; during that time Sheppey became renowned for its sheep rearing, wool trade, and cheese making, exporting annually to Rome, corn, wool, cheese, oysters and pearls. The oyster beds were at Shellness, from which it derives its name.

The Romans withdrew from England in the year 410 A.D. after five hundred years of occupation, and for many years civil war and a state of anarchy prevailed. The Saxons settled in Sheppey and fortified the island, changing the name to "Scaepige".

Kent was divided into five divisions called 'Lathes'. To enable a more complete system of justice to be administered, the lathes were divided into 'Hundreds', of which many years later became Towns and Boroughs. Sheppey was incorporated into the 'Hundred of Milton' in the 'Lathe of Scray'.

The Saxon King, Ecombert, was the grandson of King Ethelbert and Queen Bertha, the daughter of the King of Paris. Bertha was a devout christian and converted her husband to that faith and Ethelbert became the first christian King of Kent. When Ecombert became king in 640 A.D. he married Sexburga, the daughter of Annas, King of East Anglia who was also a devout christian, Ecombert became converted to christianity and upon his death in 663 A.D. Queen Sexburga built an abbey to commemorate him. The Isle of Sheppey was given to her by her son Egbert. King of Kent, for this purpose. The monastery was built on the highest point of the Island, originally called Cyningburg, Sexburga renamed it Monasterium Scapeiae and endowed it for 77 nuns.

The Monastery was dedicated in 675 A.D. and Queen Sexburga became its first Abbess. Upon the death of her sister Ethelfrida, who founded the monastery at Ely, Sexburga became Abbess of Ely and her daughter Erminelda became Abbess of Minster, she in her turn was followed by her daughter Werburga. These four holy women of noble birth were all canonised, Sexburga was canonised in 709 A.D. and Minster became a place of pilgrimage.

For over one hundred years the Abbey prospered and the Island became civilised. Then came the marauding Norsemen in 798 and again in 852 A.D., the beautiful Abbey was destroyed and the nuns put to the sword. The invaders became more powerful and by 858 Sheppey was dominated by them and remained so for forty years, by the year 895 they resolutely came to stay.

The Danish Prince, Hoestan, fortified Minster and built a fort at "Scipe" (Shurland) and another at Queenborough. After his defeat at the battle of Farnham by King Alfred he retreated to Sheppey to reorganise his forces. Once again King Alfred was victorious in battle and Hoestan fled to Sheppey. Subsequently he embraced christianity and settled there.

King Alfred died in 901 A.D. and was succeeded by Edward the Martyr, and the succession followed from father to son during eight reigns, all of whom held the title 'Earls of Sheppey'. In 979, the Danes were still troublesome and famine and plague ravished the land.

King Ethelred levied the 'Danegeld' tax in 991 hoping to bribe the Danes to leave the country; they did not go, however, so he ordered a general massacre. Sheppey did her part by murdering all the Danish invaders on the island.

King Sweyne avenged this by invading England and victoriously crowned King of England in 1014. His son Cnut (Canute) visited Sheppey and mutilated hostages by cutting off their noses and hands. He succeeded his father to the throne and lived at Shurland during part of his reign.

The Abbey was restored and more civilised conditions prevailed during the subsequent reigns of Harold I and Hardicanute who died without issue and was succeeded by Edward the Confessor.

Edward was married to Editha, the daughter of the powerful Earl Godwin. When the Earl quarelled with the King he broke into open rebellion and seized Sheppey and devastated it; once again the Abbey suffered partial demolition. Earl Godwin, however, made peace with the

King in 1053 before his death.

Edward the Confessor died without issue in 1066, and Harold II, son of Earl Godwin, was chosen to be King. William of Normandy contested the claim and invaded England, defeating Harold at the battle of Hastings on 14th October 1066.

On Christmas Day in Westminster Abbey William was crowned King.

After the battle, Harold's wife Edith (Editha of the Swan Neck) fled to Minster Abbey seeking sanctuary, for she possessed land in Sheppey and had received her education in the Abbey.

William installed his barons in important positions and into Sheppey came De Northwode, De Cobham, De Shurland, De Scepig, De Sauvage, De Peyforer and De Fiennes. All these became the principle actors in the history of Sheppey.

Domesday Book was compiled and Sheppey being the private possession of Harold, was pounced upon and devided among these Norman barons.

De Shurland built a fortified manor house on the site of the old castle of Scipe - renaming it Shurland. De Borstle built Borstal Hall (later to be renamed Gilbert Hall), De Fiennes built Sayes Court Harty and De Sauvage settled in Rushenden.

All Saxon nuns were expunged and Sheppey was ruled remorsely; the Abbey was made over to foreign nuns, all the of the Saxon heptarchy were dismissed and banished, the nuns from Newington Priory were sent to Minster after their Prioress was found murdered and the Priory given over to a monastic order.

In the year 1097 a mighty marine upheaval washed away vast portions of Kent and Essex including parts of Sheppey.

The estates of the Earl Godwin at Deal were overwhelmed and swept away in a single night. The place is now known as the treacherous Godwin Sands.

In 1096 the Lord of Sheppey was Jordanus de Sheppey of Northwolde Manor, Northwolde (now Norwood) was one of a score of manors originally held by Alnod the Kentishman, reputed son of King Harold and Edith Swannaschelles, (Edith Swan neck).

Alnod Cilt was kept as a hostage by William the Norman after the death of Harold. He was released by William Rufus and went on a pilgrimage to the Holy Land, he changed his name to Jordanus de Sheppey, reclaiming lands near his mother's retreat in Minster Abbey, his son, Stephen, took the name of Northwoode and thus founded the Norwood family of Sheppey.

The house is still occupied. Roger Northwood, the son of Stephen, accompanied King Richard I on the third crusade as his standard bearer.

In the year 1130, William de Corbeuil, Archbishop of Canterbury visited all the religious houses in his diocese. Minster was in a ruinous condition; he ordered it to be rebuilt and the monastery restored. By this time Minster had grown into a small township and the need of a place of worship was felt.

The Archbishop decided that a parish church be added to the Nun's chapel. Two monks were appointed from Augustine's Abbey Canterbury, one as a vicar to the Parish Church and the other as chaplain to the monastery. They lodged together in the east gable of the gatehouse until Parsonage Farm Minster was built to house the parish priest.

When the restoration was completed, the Abbey was rededicated as the Minster Church of St. Mary and St. Sexburga, it flourished throughout the reigns of King Stephen and Henry II. King Henry granted the rental of Rushenden and the tithes and dues of Westlands to Christ Church Canterbury.

During the reign of King Henry III (1216 - 1272), Robert de Shurland accompanied Prince Edward on a crusade in 1271, and when Edward became king he created Robert a Knight Banneret for gallantry at Caeverlock in 1300.

It was around this Robert de Shurland that the legend of Grey Dolphin is woven. Robert was a very short man with a violent temper and it is said that one day when returning to Shurland Hall he came upon a group of mourners in the churchyard who were arguing with the priest. Upon dismounting Robert enquired the cause of this unseemly conduct and was told that the priest had refused to inter the corpse unless he was paid beforehand.

Lord Robert's temper flared and in a rage he drew his great sword "Tickle Toby" and slew the priest. When he reached Shurland he had great misgivings, for it was an offence to murder a priest.

He knew that when the news reached Canterbury he would be excommunicated and severely punished, so he resolved to see the King at once.

The King's ship was anchored out to sea where he had been reviewing his fleet. He saddled his powerful horse, Grey Dolphin, rode to the sea-shore and swam far out to sea to the ship.

The King was impressed by this feat and having a great liking for Robert de Shurland he granted a pardon.

When reaching the shore again he was accosted by an old woman known as the Witch of Scrapsgate. She, having no liking for the Baron, cursed him and said "This horse which this day your life has saved, will cause your life to end". Upon this the Baron flew into a rage and once again drawing his sword he killed the faithful Grey Dolphin.

Some time later he was walking along the shore with his companions and seeing the carcase of the old horse lying there he related the tale and contemptuously kicked the skull, a bone pierced his great toe and caused blood poisoning very soon afterwards he died - thus was the old witch's prophecy fulfilled.

His death occured in 1310 and his tomb is in Minster Church; the head of Grey Dolphin rising from the waves rests by his side and for many years the horse's head surmounted the weather vane and the church was known to mariners as the 'Horse Church', being a landmark at the mouth of the Estury.

During the reign of Edward II, John de Northwood was prominent in Sheppey and two fine brasses of him and his wife Joan de Badesmere dating about 1319-20 are to be found in the church.

King Edward III thought much of the Island and commanded a castle to be built on the site of the old Saxon remains at Queenborough. It was completed in 1361. The castle was designed by William de Wykham, Bishop of Winchester, the King's architect, and built under the supervision of John Gibbon, ancestor of Edward Gibbon the celebrated historian. The Gibbon family lived for generations at Rushenden Manor, Being descended from the Lords Saye and Selle and the Crowmers of Borstall Hall.

King Edward III and his wife Queen Phillippa of Hainault resided for a time in the castle. He granted a charter in 1368, converting the lands around into a free Borough transforming the tiny fishing village of Bynne and Minster marshes into a corporate town and in honour of his Queen renamed it Reginaburgia or Queenborough. The church was built in 1363 and the King granted a charter in 1369 for the borough to become a 'Wool

Staple' for the export of wool. He envisaged the growth of a thriving port but this dream never materialized.

The customs on wool, skins and leather were formerly called Hereditory Customs of the Crown, and were due only on the export of these three staple commodities which were obliged to be brought to those ports where the King's Staple was established in order to be rated and exported. The 'Staple' industry lasted for centuries at Queenborough, the only other Staple in Kent was Canterbury.

The old Woolpack Inn at Iwade is a reminder of these days for it was a port of call for the wool carriers as they wended their way across the marshes to Queenborough.

The first Constable of Queenborough Castle was Sir John de Foxley, it is said that it was he who brought the olive wood wand from the Holy Land (now enclosed in a silver case) which has been used since then at Mayoral meetings as a staff of office.

The second Constable of Queenborough was John of Gaunt, Duke of Lancaster, and third son of King Edward III. He resigned this position in 1385 to become Regent to the young King Richard II.

Among the property aquired by John of Gaunt was Rushenden Manor, Neats Court and Danly Farm. The revenues from Rushenden and Danly Farm were granted in perpetuity to the hospital of St Katherine, it remained in their hands until 1898 when it was purchased by a local gentleman, the title on the agreement was "the Grant of John of Gaunt and others, dated 4th February Richard II (1392-8), of the Manor of Ryshynden and certain other lands in the Isle of Sheppey". This is the only title and a dispensation from Queen Victoria was required before the sale could take place.

In later years John of Gaunt quarreled with the King and was banished from the Kingdom with his son, Henry Bolingbroke.

The King became increasingly unpopular and when his uncle died he refused to allow Henry to return to claim his inheritance.

Henry raised an army abroad and invaded England to seize the throne. Richard was taken prisoner and died in captivity.

Henry was crowned King Henry IV in 1399, inheriting his father's Sheppey estates he took a great interest in the Island and did much to improve it. In 1406 Henry and his Queen made a long stay at Queenborough Castle to avoid a plague which had broken out in London;

He ordered a better road to be made from Tremod Ferry to Sockels and granted the right to collect tolls for three years for the upkeep of the roads and ferry.

The levies were ... Every strange horseman in or out of the Island 1d, every footman 1/2d, every horse loaded 1d, and unloaded 1/2d. The road was widened to the width of two pack-horses and much used by pilgrims visiting the shrine of Saint Sexburga.

The tolls were abolished on 2nd July 1929, after being in existence for 473 years.

King Henry V spent most of his time fighting in France; William de Northwoode of Norwood Manor fought with the King at Angincourt and Harfleur and was knighted for gallantry in 1415.

Henry VI became King when only one year old; a Regency was proclaimed and his uncles Humphrey, Duke of Gloucester, and John, Duke of Bedford ruled the country.

In 1423, William Cromer of Borstall Hall was appointed Lord Mayor of London for the second time.

In 1430, Eastchurch Church was in ruins and William Cheyne obtained a grant from King Henry VI to give land on which to build a new one. The licence was granted and from this date the Parish of Eastchurch was formed. The church was dedicated in 1432 and William Nudds, the architect became its first Vicar.

In 1450 Jack Cade's rebellion broke out and he attacked London.

The Duke of Buckingham, Constable of Queenborough Castle was taken prisoner and beheaded along with Sir James Fiennes of Rushenden Manor and William Cromer of Borstall Hall.

Cade attacked Queenborough Castle but was defeated and later captured, among his followers were John Cheyne of Shurland, also the Mayor of Queenborough and ten other men from Sheppey.

In 1461 Edward IV, became King and appointed John de Northwoode Constable of Queenborough Castle. In 1465, however, he resigned in favour of George, Duke of Clarence, who received the governorship of Sheppey.

In 1485, Henry Tudor, Duke of Richmond, did battle with King Richard III at Bosworth Field. His standard bearer was Sir John Cheyne of Shurland and Burke relates that "Sir John Cheyne of Shurland, and eminent soldier under the banner of the Earl of Richmond at Bosworth

Field personally encountering King Richard III was felled to the ground by the monarch, had his crest struck off and his head laid bare; for some time it is said, he remained stunned, but recovering after a while, he cut the skull and horns off the hide of an ox which chanced to be near, and fixed them on his head to supply the loss of the upper part of his helmet; he then returned to the field of battle, and did such signal service that Henry, being proclaimed King, assigned Cheyne for crest the "Bull's Cap" which his descendants still bear."

The "Bull's Cap" is incorporated in the arms of Cheyne and can be seen on the tomb of Sir Thomas Cheyne in Minster church.

The tomb of Sir John Cheyne is in Sailsbury Cathedral, he died on the 30th November 1499 and having no issue his nephew Sir Thomas Cheyne succeeded him.

King Henry VIII succeeded his father and during his reign the dissolution of the monasteries took place.

The ancient Abbey of Minster was disolved and the lands, farms, windmill and all appurtances were sold to Sir Thomas Cheyne for a small fee. Sir Thomas was a great favourite of the King, who showered him with gifts and properties during his reign.

The great house of shurland was re-built and Henry VIII accompanied by Anne Bolyn, paid a state visit to Sir Thomas Cheyne, at the time of their visit there were 400 retainers living at Shurland.

Sir Thomas Cheyne was succeeded by his only son Henry, created Lord Henry Cheyne by Queen Elizabeth, he abandoned the ancestral home of Shurland, exchanging it for land elsewhere.

He sold the site of the Abbey and manor lands together with the gatehouse to Sir Humphrey Gilbert, demolishing the Abbey and removing the stones to Berkshire where he built a house at Tuddington, the ancestral home of his mother.

Queen Elizabeth made two visitations to this newly built mansion, and Lord Henry, determined to outdo his illustrious father, spent lavishly and squandered all his father's great wealth, selling manor after manor, he lived a spendthrift and died a pauper, leaving no issue, so ended the Cheyne family of Sheppey.

With the closing of Shurland, Sheppey became neglected and the Queen endevoured to bring back prosperity by issueing an export licence for the manufacture of leather goods, this, however, was not a success. A small garrison was installed at Shurland for the defence of the Island.

Queenborough was now sucessful as a shipping port and wool staple and in 1579 the first record of a chemical works in this country was made. Mathias Falconer, a Fleming, was the first person to discover iron pyrites in great abundance on the beach between Warden and Minster, he built a small factory at Queenborough for the manufacture of sulphate of iron.

It is from this original factory that the Queenborough Chemical works developed.

By the act of Parliament passed in 1576, the Court of Hustings held beneath the old Court Tree in the Manor of Kingsborough, was empowered to levy a rate on the inhabitants of Sheppey for "the maintenance of the Queen's Ferry," and "to collect any revenues arising, for the better communications with the mainland."

William Cromer of Borstall Hall, who had been imprisoned in the Tower for ten years for his share in the Wyatt rebellion was released. He died later in 1598 and is buried at Tunstall, he left no issue; and thus after 200 years ended the House of Cromer in Minster.

Queen Elizabeth is believed to have been the guest of Sir Edward Hoby at Queenborough Castle in 1582; during her reign she took a great deal of interest in the welfare of the Island.

The Queen died on March 24th 1603 and bequeathed the Crown to James Stuart, James IV of Scotland. It was Lord Hunsdon, Lord of the Manor of Kingsborough in Sheppey who was sent as a special messenger to Scotland to inform the King of his accession to the English throne.

Shurland Hall, which since the death of Henry Cheyne had been vested on the Crown was given by the King to Sir Phillip Herbert, K.B. who was greated Baron Herbert of Shurland, Earl of Pembroke and Montgomery, which titles are still in existance, the King gave to Sir Herbert many of the Cheyne possessions including Shurland, Norwood, Cale Hill, and Leysdown Manor. He was the last Constable of Queenborough Castle.

In Sheppey, new landowners were in possession, Sir Richard Butler , Sir Thomas Finch, Sir Julius Caesar and Sir Paul Bayning were some of the men who replaced the old nobility.

During the reign of James I land drainage was carried out and road improvements made. The Manor of Minster and site of the Abbey was sold to Henry Richards Esq. who left it to Gabriel Livesey of Parsonage Farm, Eastchurch.

King James I died in 1625 and was succeeded by the ill fated Charles I who married Princess Henrietta Maria, the daughter of King Henri IV of France. The estate of the Manor of Neats Court was settled on her as a marriage dower, it then consisted of some 640 acres. After the Civil War it was given by the King's Trustees to Sir Edward Hales.

The King became very unpopular and when in 1634-36 he levied "Ship Money" on the estates of his subjects many of them rebelled and refused to pay. Among the knights who resented this notorious tax was Sir Michael Livesey of Parsonage Farm, Eastchurch, who joined forces with Cromwell and commanded the Roundheads of the Kentish Horse.

Sir Michael Livesey with Agustine Garland, the Member of Parliament for Queenborough, were two of the regicides who signed the death warrant of Charles I.

During the Protectorship of Cromwell Sheppey suffered considerably. Belonging as it did to the Crown, all the manors held "in Capite" by knights service were valued and vested under Cromwell and all revenues were applied to "General Purposes". The Lords were depived of their privileges and dispossessed of all military and civil power, and all historical records were destroyed. Churches were stripped of their treasures and the tombs of the early noblemen were violated and broken; a few, however, were hidden and rediscovered some two centuries later.

The Manors of Minster, Shurland, Rushenden, Kingsborough, Norwood, Neats Court, Calehill and Queenborough shared the same fate. Chivalry and Feudal bonds were dissipated, Shurland Hall was partially destroyed but Queenborough Castle was demolished entirely in 1650. The stone and timbers were sold for building material.

With the castle demolished, the Manors dismantled and the small garrisons provided by the former Lords disbanded, Sheppey was rendered useless for defence purposes for the first time since the Norman Conquest.

In 1658, after years of oppresive rule, Oliver Cromwell died and in 1660, the exiled King Charles II returned in triumph to England. Upon the restoration of the monarchy the regicides, Livesey and Garland, fled the country, Agustine Garland was captured and brought to trial, he was deported and sold into slavery in Tangiers. Michael Livesey escaped to Holland but was recognised by some Kentish men and put to death.

The estates of both were confiscated by the Crown; Parsonage Farm, the home of the Livesey's for generations was given to James, Duke of York, later to become King James II.

Charles II, recognising the helpless condition of the Island, endevoured to put it into a better state of defence and ordered a new fortification and dockyard to be built.

Accompanied by his chief engineer, Sir Bernard de Gomme, Sir William Brockman and Samuel Pepys, his Naval Administrators, he visited the Island to lay out the plans on August 18th 1665.

The King made two more visits to the Island to inspect the progress and his brother, James, Duke of York, made a prolonged stay in Sheppey to inspect the new dockyard in 1669.

He stayed at Neats Court and Holm Place during the visit.

Meanwhile the Dutch were preparing for invasion and England was ill prepared for war.

On June 16th 1667, the Dutch fleet advanced to the mouth of the Thames, burning houses and barns on the Essex coast. Sir Edward Spragg was in command of the garrison and dockyard. DE Ruyter had seventy two ships of the line and frigates, besides armed transports, fire ships, sloops and galleons, having on board some 2,790 troops.

At 4 P.M. on Sunday June 9th, Van Ghent's division proceeded towards the Lower Hope. It reached Hole Haven in Sea Reach the wind having subsided. Sir Edward Spragg sent for reinforcements from the Monmouth, only forty four sailors put in an appearance, the rest deserted. The ill prepared fort was abandoned, after one man was killed and another wounded and seven of the guns dismantled.

Under cover of fire the Dutch landed with 800 men and took possession of the fort. Looting all they could lay hands on, they quitted the fort after laying that and all the adjoining land under water.

On June 11th 1667, Sheerness was lost to the Dutch. The Mayor of Queenborough, in order to prevent bloodshed, ordered the town to surrender, and the Dutch flag was hoisted over the town hall - the only place in England which had ever had the flag of a foreign invader flying over it since the Norman conquest.

Sheppey was held by the Dutch for eleven days, in which time they took possession of hulks and stores looting and carrying off thousands of sheep and cattle, the estimated value of which exceeded £40,000.

The Dutch proceeded to Chatham after forcing the chain boom

stretched across the Medway below Gillingham, they succeeded in passing Upnor Castle and captured and destroyed several of our finest men-war. The Royal Charles and Unity were captured, the loyal London, Royal Oak, Royal James, Mathias, Charles V, and Sancta Maria were burned. The Marmaduke, Victory, Royal Katherine and St George were sunk. We also lost some fire ships and ketches and roughly some 1,500 men.

The Dutch lost three men-o-war, some fire ships and 150 men killed and as many wounded.

Samuel Pepys with many others fled from London on 12th June 1667 taking with him his wife and his father and some £1,300 in gold.

The Dutch proceeded to Chatham then slowly retired and hovered around the Nore then finally departed to return again on 23rd July. They were then engaged by Sir Edward Spragg who defeated them and drove them out to sea.

The immediate result of this invasion was that the principal land owners vacated their seats and surrendered their Crown lands and left Sheppey for good.

King Charles made a treaty with the Dutch and then turned his attention to restoring the garrision and dockyard.

On 23rd June 1668, the King, accompanied by Prince Rupert, visited the Island. It was decided to rebuild the fort at once, the corporation of the City of London voted a sum of £10,000 for this purpose.

Upon the death of Charles in 1685, James, Duke of York, became King James II; he owned several manors and estates on Sheppey and paid a number of visits to the Island in which he had always shown great interest. The draining of the marshes took place during his reign .

King James II was a devout catholic and became much disliked, discontent became rife and a revolution was pending.

The people turned towards his protestant daughter Mary and her husband, William of Orange. They visited England in 1688, escorted by a large army. The King, deserted by his generals, sent the Queen and infant prince to France, pretending to follow them, he stayed in disguise with Sir Edward Hales at Neats Court from whence they went to Elmely where they boarded a hoy to take them to France. However, they were captured at Shellness and taken to Faversham, from there they were escorted to London. Later the King was allowed to abdicate; he came to Rochester from there he took passage to Queenborough and from that port sailed to France on Christmas eve 1688.

Sir Edward Hales of Neats Court was imprisoned in the Tower for eighteen months; upon his release he joined the King in exile and died in 1695, his body was interred in the church of St. Suplice in Paris.

The King died in Rome in 1701, at the age if 68, his tomb is in St. Peter's Rome.

In 1699, Sir John Banks of Rushenden Manor died, his daughter and sole heir had married Mr Henage Finch. Thus the ancient Manor passed into the hands of the Finch family.

Henage Finch gained many honours, and in 1703 was created Baron Geurnsey and later Earl of Aylesford. His son Henage, inherited the estates and transferred Rushenden to his brother John.

Upon the death of William and Mary, Queen Anne reigned.

She was the last of the Stuarts and the first monarch to be styled Sovriegn of Great Britain. Upon her death George I succeeded to the throne, being the great grandson of James I.

In 1708, the dry dock at Sheerness was completed, at this date there was no town at all ... a few houses near the dockyard and at Blue Town, some government residences in the garrison for the Goverener and a few officers and just enough men to man the fort, this consisted the town.

Many of the workmen travelled from Chatham by boat each day, so the goverment decided to utilise the old men-o-war which were used as breakwaters, for lodging the men.

John Welsey describes them in his journal, there was a King Street, Queen Street, Princess Street and many more, all connected with each other by gangways. In every street was a midwife with name plate prominantly displayed. The forebears of many Sheppey inhabitants were born aboard these old hulks.

During the reign of George II many manors changed hands and 'Pocket Boroughs' were formed.

In 1732, William Hogarth, the painter, made a perigrination to Sheppey with five companions, making sketches and writing verses on their adventures. They stayed at an inn in Queenborough, now numbers 23 and 24 High Street. A sketch made by Hogarth can be seen in the Guildhall, Queenborough.

In 1752, Mr. Edward Jacobs F.R.S. of Faversham, purchased Nutts

Manor at Leysdown and came to live there; he was a notable antiquarian and naturlist and discovered many interesting fossils and rare plants and wrote a book on the Flowers and Fauna of Sheppey.

In January 1756, a large whale was caught at Scrapsgate, it measured 36 feet long 22 feet wide and 8 feet from eyes to tip of nose. It yielded 20 hogshead of oil. Stephen Rouse of Minster recorded this in his diary, he also made a detailed water colour sketch of the whale on the beach, this sketch is still extant.

During the reign of George III Sheppey endured several artic winters. The Nore Lightship was driven out to sea and ice stretched from Sheppey to Essex as far as the 'Red Sand'. The London passage boats and the ferry boat were frozen up for several days and thousands of lobsters and whelks were frozen on the beach, Stephen Rouse records that "they were delicious to eat".

In 1797 both the French and the Dutch threatened invasion, Lord Nelson's rise to fame took place whilst he was stationed at Sheerness. He lived in the house next to Queenborough Church when stationed here, and was a regular communicant at Queenborough Church.

In the Eastchurch parish register of 1796, is an interesting record. "Oct. 23rd, Grace, wife of Isaac Davis, drowned herself in the Old House Pond". In the affidavit we learn that she "was duly buried in woollen". This was in strict accordance with an Act of Parliament passed in 1666, and was rigoursly enforced, with the avowed object of "protecting and encouraging woollen manufacture, and of the prevention of the exportation of moneys for the buying and importing of linen".

It was even enacted that the quilting round the inside of the coffin and the bandage round the feet of the corpse should be of the same material as the shroud; and to secure this end, before a defunct person could obtain sepulture it was necessary for mourners to produce an affidavit sworn before a resident Juctice of the Peace, to the effect that the Act of Parliament had been duly complied with.

There are many such affidavits in the old church registers but this one is interesting because the Old House Pond is reputed to have been haunted by the ghost of a woman on Oct. 23rd each year and was known locally as the Haunted Pond.

Some years ago, however, the ancient half-timbered house was demolished and the pond made into a car park.

In 1797, the Mutiny at the Nore broke out and the islanders lived in terror of Richard Parker and his 15,000 mutineers, remaining in a state of seige until 15th June of that year when the mutiny was crushed and the leader, Richard Parker, and many others were hanged, after being found guilty of treason.

Meanwhile the Dutch were still waiting for an opportunity to invade, but Admiral Duncan defeated them at the battle of Camperdown and they were put to flight after heavy losses, and Sheppey was spared another invasion.

The nineteenth century dawned with another threat of danger for Napoleon Buonaparte was preparing to invade England.

Panic reigned and on the 6th July 1803, a bill was hurriedly passed for the purpose of augmenting our auxilliary forces for National Defence to the extent of 70,000 men, to be called The Army Reserve for Home Defence, (the first Home Guard).

All males between the age of 18 and 45 years were liable to be called upon to serve, the selection to be determined by local ballot. Another Act was passed for the purpose of arming and training all unmarried men between the age of 17 and 30 years.

The room at the back of the Crown Inn was their headquarters. Minster was called upon to provide nine men called "Quota Men" to serve in the reserve. Thirty seven persons who were liable to serve were duly called upon and paid the Overseers of the parish one guinea each to be exempted from service. The overseers then proceeded to find substitutes at a cost of £251-10-0 for County money and £55-4-11 additional expenses.

The Lord of the Manor of Borstal Hall, Mr. W. Swift with the church wardens and overseers of Minster, caused a rate to be levied in September 1803 of sixpence in the pound, "A tax rate upon all and every inhabitant in the Parish of MInster under the Act passed in the 44th year of the reign of King George III, instituted an Act for establishing and maintaining a permanant aditional force for the defence of the Realm for the purpose of raising two hundred and twenty pounds per man, by fine as by precept from the County Court and in pursuance of the Act".

This rate continued throughout the Peninsular War and was withdrawn only after the fall of Napoleon in 1815.

On May 5th 1800, a land slip occured in Sheppey. A huge tract of land about 500 ft long and 150 ft wide gave way between the cliffs of Warden and Leysdown slid gradually down to the sea, taking with it part of a house, barns and outbuildings. No lives or cattle were lost, it was so gradual that the land planted with corn was undisturbed and was harvested in good condition the following Summer. The deep valley made by the landslide is known as 'Busby Hole'.

Smuggling was rife in Sheppey, the head quarters of the Sheppey gang were at the Royal Oak inn at the bottom of Oak Lane, Minster and an inn called "The Smack Aground" at Warden, now long since disappeared into the sea.

In 1814, great inprovements were made at the dockyard and the foundation stone of Admiralty House was laid. It was built as a residence for William, Duke of Clarence, who was stationed at Sheerness, he was afterwards known when he came to the throne as the Sailor King, William 1V. This is the last record of a Prince of the Blood Royal residing in Sheppey. The work of re-building the dockyard was undertaken by John Rennie, the great civil engineer, he supervised the construction until he died in 1821, the work was completed by John Rennie, the younger, on 5th September 1823. The new dockyard was opened by the Duke of Clarence.

William 1V became king on 26thJune 1830, and in 1832, under the great Reform Bill Queenborough became disenfranchised and could no longer send two Members of Parliament annually, which it had been privileged to do since the reign of Queen Elizabeth. One of the last contestants was Sir Thomas Gladstone, the brother of William Gladstone, Prime Minster.

Cholera broke out in Sheppey and lasted for over two years.

The mortality rate was so high that the parish meadow at Eachchurch was requisitioned as a mass burial ground.

One of the victims was Vice Admiral Sir Richard King, K.C.B. Commander in Chief at the Nore. He was a great commander under Lord Nelson, his tomb is in All Saints Church, Eastchurch.

In 1837, Queen Victoria succeeded to the throne and during her reign all churches in Sheppey were restored, schools were built also Holy Trinity Church, St. Pauls Bluetown, The Catholic Church and the second Dockyard Church, land development took place and scores of workmen's dwellings were erected, the dockyard prospered as never before.

Queenborough had now become an important port for passengers and freight bound for the Continent, twice a day steamers sailed to Flushing, Belgium and Holland, this service continued until 1922, when it was transferred to Harwich.

In 1887, to celebrate Queen Victoria's Diamond Jubilee, a stained glass window depicting St. Sexburga holding a model of Minster Abbey was placed in Minster Church.

On 18th July 1860, the railway connecting Sheppey to the rest of the world was opened - no longer need the inhabitants of the Island travel in Prattens Van to the mainland, waiting on the 'Hard' until the ferryman decided to take them across, it was a slow progress. No wonder there was tremendous rejoicing - they now had a bridge and a railway and everyone could visit the great world beyond the Swale.

The Queen died in1901 and was succeeded by King Edward VII.

The Inhabitants of Sheppey erected the town clock to commemorate his coronation. Between 1902 and 1904 the Sheppey Light Railway was opened, operating between Queenborough and Leysdown, it became very popular with Londoners who were discovering Sheppey as a seaside resort. Electric trams also were now running from Bluetown to East Minster.

In 1903 a new water works was built at Minster, the digging uncovered many relics of the past. Two fine efigies, some Saxon coffin lids and a great quantity of prehistoric fossils were discovered. The spring from which the water was drawn is 600 feet below the surface.

King George V succeeded his father in 1910 and in 1911 - 12 Eastchurch became the cradle of aviation in England. The brothers Short set up a small factory first at Leysdown then moving to Stone Pitts farm, Eastchurch and when Germany declared war in 1914 Sheppey's defences included an aerodrome.

Troops were stationed at Shurland Hall and in all the Manor houses during the war. On November 26th 1914, the battleship Bulwark was blown up in Sheerness harbour owing to an internal combustion.

On 22nd May 1915, another tragic explosion took place when the minelayer Princess Irene suffered the same fate and even greater loss of life.

In 1929, the Nore Lightship which had guarded the Estuary since 1793, was declared redundant; it's beam, however, could still be seen in 1934.

Leysdown started catering for campers, Nutts Farm allocated a meadow and hired out sleeping tents, other landowners quickly followed and a thriving camping industry was born.

Excursion trains ran from London direct to Sheerness at 2/8 return fare, and Sheppey became a popular seaside resort for East Londoners.

Since the reign of King Henry IV in 1402, the right to collect tolls at the King's Ferry had been enforced and on the 2nd July 1929 after 572 years, the toll was abolished, and free access to Sheppey was established, which added considerably to the growth of the Island.

The aerodrome at Eastchurch had rapidly developed and when the second world war broke out it was very important base.

Sheppey was declared a closed area and a pass was necessary for the inhabitants to enter and leave the Island.

A boom defence barrier was placed across the mouth of the Estuary from the Royal Oak to Shoeburyness and concrete forts were placed in the sea at strategic points, these had a devastating effect later on the 'Doodle Bugs' before they reached London.

In 1940, Eastchurch aerodrome suffered a severe bombing attack during the Battle of Britain and a Pilot boat was blown up by a mine which had somehow slipped past the boom.

All unoccupied houses were taken over by the army.

Ack-Ack batteries were set up everywhere, the beaches were covered with barbed wire and concrete pill-boxes adorned the esplanade.

The R.A.F. regiment was stationed along the cliffs from Leysdown to Minster.

On the evening of 17th June 1944, a great fleet of ships and Mulbury Harbours could be seen stretching from the boom defence to the mouth of the Thames in preparation for the invasion of Cherbourg, in the light of dawn next morning nothing could be seen except the masts of a ship leaning drunkenly against the horizon.

This was the Richard Montgomery, an American ship on 'Lease Loan' loaded with ammunition, she had slipped her moorings and had drifted on to a sand bank and stuck fast. Over the years this wreck has caused a great deal of controversy, but it still can be seen although not much remains visible.

After the war Leysdown became increasingly popular as a holiday resort and from those first few tents it has grown into a chalet town, some 30,000 people live there during the Summer.

The water supplies were quite inadequate and in 1960 a new resevoir was opened; since then larger water pipes have been installed, many roads were made up and street lighting improved.

Leysdown railway was closed in 1948-9 and the aerodrome became a transit camp for displaced Indians in 1947 when India gained her independance. After that it became the first open prison in England.

A striking war memorial was erected at Eastchurch and was unveiled by the founder of the old aero club in 1901, Mr. Moore Brabazon, now Lord Brabazon of Tara.

In February 1953, a great flood damaged much of Sheerness.

The year 1960 was a memorable one for the Island, two important events took place, the first had a widespread effect on the Island for on March 31st 1960 the dockyard was declared redundant and officially closed. For 300 years the dockyard had provided the livlihood of Sheppey, now unemployment cast its dark shadow, shops, cinemas and transport suffered and there was an air of deep depression hanging over the Island.

The second event was more hopeful, for on April, 9th 1960 the new ferry bridge was opened by Princess Marina, Duchess of Kent, and at 9-50 a.m. on that day the train travelled over the old bridge for the last time.

Sheppey went through a period of unemployment and despondency after the closing of the 'Yard'; but new industries came to the Island. The dockyard was purchased by a development company and has expanded into the finest commercial docks in the south of England.

The Navy departed, and the garrison closed, Admiralty House, that imposing structure, was demolished and the last of the Dockyard Churches is now a warehouse, St. Paul's Church, Trinity School, (the first National school to be built in Sheerness), The Hippodrome, and the boy's Technical School in the Broadway have gone , almost all of the ancient historical buildings have now disappeared, even the Tower Clock was threatened but the indignant citizens protested so vigorously that it has been allowed to remain in situ.

In March 1971, a large new Comprehensive School was opened in Minster by the young Duchess of Kent; it was one of the most modern of its kind and put Sheppey in the forefront of education in Kent. In 1974, Sheppey became part of the Swale District Council, as a result the ancient Borough of Queenborough has lost its status and its Mayor.

Sheppey's future prosperity lies in the expansion of its industries and continuing efforts to attract new trades. The holiday camps provide seasonable work for many people; new and better class houses are being built, the Oulau Line operates a modern service daily to Holland and efforts are being made to attract tourists to the Island.

We hope that Sheppey can now look forward to a future of greater hope and prosperity.

2 THE HISTORY OF MINSTER

Saxon Monasterium.   Domesday Rolls.   Sexburga Mynster.
Menstre.   Minster.

The history of Minster begins with the building of Minster Abbey, as indeed does the History Of Sheppey, for Minster is the "Mother Parish" of the Island.

The Abbey was built in the years 644-675 by Queen Sexburga the widow of Ecombert, King of Kent. In those far off days, wealthy, high born ladies when left without the protection of their husbands, were a prey to any robber, baron or chieftain, so they sought protection of the Church and entered a nunnery or, if of Royal birth and extremely wealthy, they built their own nunnery as did Queen Sexburga.

Her son, King Egbert, gave to her the Isle of Sheppey for this purpose and the Abbey was built on the high ground which in those days was the centre of the Island.

The Church, Minster, Isle of Sheppy. 7.   G.E. Matthews

Almost all the monastic and hall buildings of Saxon England were made of wood, some wealthy Abbeys and Cathedrals, however, were made of stone. There is no remaining evidence of what material that Minster Abbey was made of, but in view of the fact that it was razed to the ground several times by the Danes, it could be assumed that it was a wooden structure. The 12th century re-building was definitely Kentish ragstone and caen stone.

So the great Abbey was built and we must imagine it with its refectory, dormitory, chapter house, cloisters, garth and chapel all enclosed within high walls. It housed 77 nuns and Sexburga was its first Abbess. Her daughter Erminelda succeeded her and was followed by her niece and a succession of Abbesses of noble birth.

For more than a hundred years it enjoyed a peaceful existence and a flourishing village grew up around it. Then came the danes in their longboats. Swooping down on the seaboard of Kent, they overran "Escapiae" or Sheppey, burnt down and desecrated the Abbey and had no mercy on any man.

Twice they came to Sheppey and ravaged it, the first time was in 851 AD, the second in 855. Eventually the Danes settled in England and an uneasy peace reigned. King Cnut (Canute) lived for a time in a castle which stood on the site of the later Shurland Hall. It was then called "Scipe" castle.

The Abbey again suffered destruction in the eleventh century when, in 1052 it fell prey to the banished Earl Godwin.

Then came William of Normandy and with him came his powerful barons. He gave them land in Sheppey on which to build fortified manors; to De Shurland he gave "Scipe" and upon this site he built the first Shurland Hall; De Northwoode built Northwoode Manor, now Norwood; De Fiennes built Sayes Court at Harty; De Borstal, Borstal Hall and these are a few of the names which live on in Sheppey. William found the Abbey in a ruinous state and almost empty. He transferred the nuns from Newington Abbey to Minster after their Prioress had been found murdered.

In 1130, William de Corbeuil, Archbishop of Canterbury, on his visitations of the religious in Kent, ordered Minster Abbey to be rebuilt and restored. By this time, the population had increased and a place of worship was needed; the parishioners could not use the nuns' chapel so the

Archbishop ordered a Parish Church to be built on to the nuns' chapel. Two monks were appointed from St. Augustine's, Canterbury, one as the Vicar of the Parish Church and one as Chaplain and Confessor for the Abbey.

The Gate House was rebuilt about this time and the parish priest and the Abbey priest lodged there until the Parsonage was built at Minster, now Parsonage Farm, and the parish priest took up residence there.

When the rebuilding was completed it was rededicated as the Minster Church of St. Mary and St. Sexburga, by which name, after 800 years, it is still called.

During the Middle Ages, many benefits were conferred on the Abbey by Royal Charters, and one benefactor, Sir Roger Northwoode, who died in 1286, had a great affection for the ruined church and gave much money to relieve its poverty.

Further confirmation of the Abbey's possessions and liberties was granted by successive Kings in 1377, 1399, 1413, 1485 and 1509.

All was not peace in the Abbey for complaints made by the nuns are recorded. For instance in 1343 they had been hindered from holding their yearly fair at Minster and that in 1339, the Prioress had been besieged in the Priory for five days.

Visits from the Archbishops called forth rebukes, and the nuns complained that they had no servant to serve them food or drink, there was no infirmary, the sick died in the dormitory, the gate of the cloister was closed too strictly and the Prioress gave no accounts.

The Prioress who was ordered to remedy these shortcomings was Agnes Revers.

In the year 1402, King Henry IV gave instructions that a roadway or wall was to be properly maintained from Tremmode (King's Ferry) to Minster Church and that the cost thereof should not be borne by the Court Leet. This roadway was a continuation of one leading direct from the village of Iwade along which the old pilgrims were in the habit of riding when on their way to the monastery of Minster.

A favourite halting place of the pilgrims was the Crittenden Fields, now forming a part of Scocles Farm. Although at this time the wall was only about four foot wide, just room enough for a packhorse, in latter years it was made of sufficient width to allow a cart to pass along it.

So life in Minster revolved around the Abbey until the reign of King Henry VIII who quarrelled with the Pope and took upon himself the role of head of the Church of England. To destroy the power of the Church and to replenish his coffers, he ordered the disbanding of all Abbeys, monasteries and religious houses and claimed their wealth, jewels and rich furnishings for the Crown. He ordered the destruction of the buildings, using the materials to help build castles on the coast for the defence of the realm.

The sites and the lands belonging to the monasteries he sold or gave to his favourites in exchange for other benefits.

In 1539, Minster Abbey with all its buildings, farms, windmill and appurtances were sold to Sir Thomas Cheyney of Shurland for the sum of £198. Since Sir Thomas Cheyney, along with Thomas Cromwell and several other knights was the gentleman who took all the inventories of the dissolved monasteries, the deal looks very suspicious.

Sir Thomas also acquired Faversham Abbey, Davington and several other religious houses. In that year, the tithe for the whole parish was £120 per year. The King (Henry VIII) intending to benefit the village and future vicars, required that Sir Thomas Cheyney should pay £40 per annum to the vicar, this was then one third of the total.

The last Prioress of Minster Abbey was Dame Alice Crane who received £14 per annum as a pension. The palace of the Abbess stood where the present vicarage now stands.

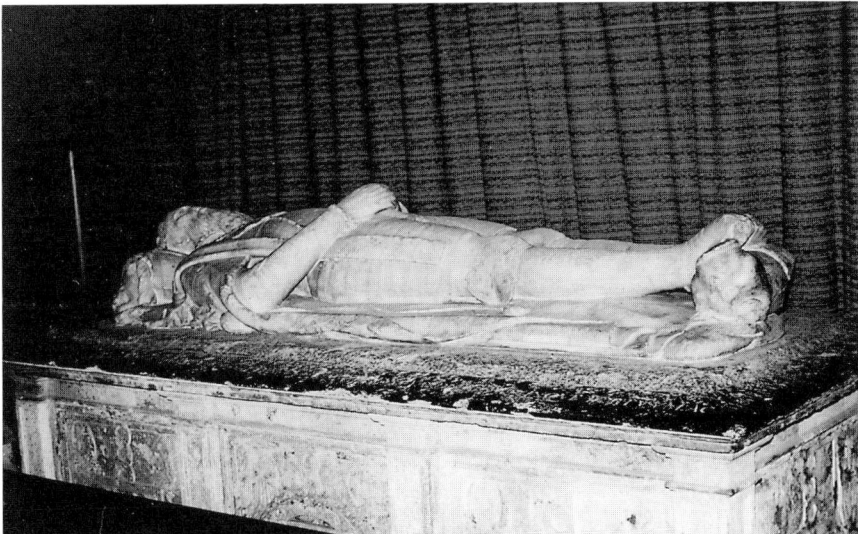

The death of Sir Thomas Cheyney in 1559 caused great changes to Minster. In his will he expresses a wish for "a tomb to be made nygh to the pace where my late wyef Frydeswyth do lye in my chapel at Minster". His tomb is in the church where it was placed when the chapel was demolished.

There lies the great man who, during his lifetime, acquired vast possessions and much wealth and in his great house of Shurland entertained King Henry VIII and Anne Boleyn, under whose patronage Minster prospered and grew yet, with all his fame and high offices, desired to be laid to rest in the small chapel at Minster.

Upon his death, his possessions passed to his son Henry who was later created Lord Henry Cheyney of Tuddington, Berkshire. This extravagant young man soon dissipated his father's wealth, exchanging Shurland Hall with Queen Elizabeth for other lands, and selling the monastery and gatehouse with the surrounding land to Sir Humphrey Gilbert.

The Abbey was dismantled and the material taken away and used to build a mansion for Lord Cheyney at Tuddington. Shurland remained empty and forsaken, the farms deserted and the tenancy neglected.

Sir Humphrey and Lady Gilbert lived in the Abbey gatehouse for many years. It was here that he planned his explorations, and his half-brother Sir Walter Raleigh and friends Sir Francis Drake and Sir Martin Frobisher often visited him at Minster.

He lived in great poverty and when he was fitting out the expedition to discover new lands, Sir Humphrey wrote many letters to the Queen begging for money owed to him to be paid. He said his wife was forced to sell the clothes off her back and, while he was away, Lady Gilbert suffered extreme poverty and received money from the parish priest to aid her.

The first expedition was a failure and Sir Humphrey Gilbert returned home to Minster to try to raise money for a further expedition. In 1583 he set off once more and was successful in discovering Newfoundland. He planted the English flag there and became its first Governor.

Sir Humphrey, however, did not live to enjoy the fruits of his labours for, on September 9th, 1583, he was lost when his small ship, the "Squirrel", foundered in a storm whilst he was exploring the coast.

Lady Gilbert retired to Maidstone and the Queen claimed the gatehouse and all the Minster lands which Sir Humphrey Gilbert had mortgaged to her. Later she gave these to Sir Edward Hoby along with the now ruined

Shurland. Sir Edward eventually sold all his Sheppey property and the Manor of Minster changed hands many times in succeeding years.

When the Cheyney chapel was dismantled, Lord Henry Cheyney removed the tombs of his ancestors into the church. Sir Robert de Shurland, his first ancestor, lies beneath an ornate canopy, originally designed it is believed for someone during the 14th century, perhaps an Abbess of noble birth. It appears that it was never finished and Sir Robert's tomb was laid to rest in the vacant place. His horse, Grey Dolphin, is by his side and recalls the legend woven around him.

The grand tomb of Sir Thomas Cheyney stands near the choir stalls.

The "Yorkist Tomb" in the nun's chapel is believed to be that of Hugh, Lord de Badlesmere, a Yorkist knight killed in the War of the Roses. The fifteenth century tomb on the floor of the north chancel is believed to be that of either Sir John Northwoode who died in 1416, or of Sir William Cheyney who died in 1441 and wished to be buried in St Katherine's chapel within the AbbeyChurch.

The unique feature of this tomb is that the praying hands hold before them a small oval medallion with the figure of a man engraved upon it, presumed represent his soul in prayer. The figure itself has been much mutilated and the feet cut away. This tomb was discovered in 1833 buried five feet down in the churchyard.

The two stone coffin lids are Saxon and probably commemorated important Abbesses of Saxon times.

The Northwoode brasses lie on the floor of the south chancel between the choir stalls. They are presumed to represent Sir John Northwoode, who died in 1319 and his wife Joan de Badlesmere, who died a year later. The brasses are of French or Flemish workmanship dating from between 1325 and 1330 and seem to have suffered various vicissitudes since they were first completed.

During the seventeenth and eighteenth centuries, Minster Church continued to play its part in the life of the Island. In 1640, the Curates stipend was £16-3-4 per year and there were 265 communicants in the parish.

In 1798, the historian, Hasted wrote that the fair on Palm Monday still continued to be held, the right to hold it had been granted in 1366 by Edward III.

This fair was held at Kingsborough where there stood a gigantic oak tree marking the boundary between the ancient Manors of Norwood and Kingsborough. Here, on every Palm Monday "Leet Court" was held where dues were paid and the ferry wardens elected. A "mop fair" was also held where servants and farm hands were hired by the farmers. Each person carried the "mark of his trade", a mop or whip, or shepherd's crook.

The selected servants were hired for a year and is from these mop fairs that "Mothering Sunday" comes. These hirelings were allowed to go home for one day each year to visit their parents, and they usually took with them a gift of a special sort of cake. This was called a "Simnel Cake" and it was eaten on Mothering Sunday, the special day for reunion with their families.

The care of the poor was the chief concern of the Church. Rates were levied for the repair of the highways, for needful repairs to the Church and also for the poor.

In 1760, the first "poor-house" was built. It was called the House of Industry and from this name we get the name of "Workhouse".

The Church also inherited a certain interest in the maintenance of order on the Island. In 1332, the Lady Prioress complained that her pillory at Minster had been cut down. Nearly five hundred years later, the Overseers and Churchwardens wrote to the whole of the publicans of this parish, in Blue Town and Mile Town especially, complaining of great irregularities: "Unless your house is completely shut up and your drinking rooms cleared of your customers during Divine Service on Sundays, your certificate will not be signed, and complaint will be made to the Magistrates".

In 1726, a young man named Stephen Rouse came to live in Minster. He was an educated, intelligent man, and acted as schoolmaster, clerk, lawyer and magistrate. The most notable fact is that he kept a diary for forty years, in these diaries he entered all the daily details of his life and thus left a valuable record of life in Minster in the 18th century.

Stephen Rouse was the owner of a small farm, believed to be 'Petfield'. He had a carpenters shop and a saddlers; he employed men to build houses and do repairs, and was evidently well to do.

In those superstitious days he was no exception, he studied astronomy and predicted storms and earthquakes, disease and famine.

Stephen Rouse seemed to be obsessed by the weather, for he records it three times daily in his diaries, every day, for forty years. He wrote in a small precise hand with quill pens and ink which he himself made.

Some entries here are quoted, "3rd June 1773, Captain Phipps sailed from Sheerness to find the N.W. Passage" ... "1773. The newly built Malt-house was used for the first time. Caught 853 flounders at 'Cole-hole' - gave to seventeen members of the poor- house."

"August 2nd 1775. On this day the first wheat was ground in the new mill at Minster."

"1775. Shingled Church spire ..." "Jan: 1776. Severe frost, ice at King's Ferry 5" thick, people crossed over the ferry - a butcher drove his sheep across, the previous great freeze was in 1684. In February the ice had to be cut away for the ferry to operate."

March 17th. 1778, Press gang busy.

April 25th, King George III visited the Nore in Lord Sandwich's yacht - viewed H.M.S Victory and six ships of the Line - on Monday visited Sheerness Dockyard.

1778. Soldiers came to start a new garrison ... planted pineapple and tobacco.

1781. Four soldiers camped in Hundred Acres (where the Catholic Church and Seaview Hotel now stand).

1782. Battle at the 'Highlander' between soldiers with drawn bayonets and the inhabitants ... went to the garrison to see the Captain ... soldiers reprimanded.

May 1782. Corn under water ... June influenza starts ... Sept. Grand Fleet sailed for Gibraltar.

1789. Severest frost, one continuous sheet of ice from Sheppey to Essex. Nore Lightship carried out to sea ... whelks and lobsters in great quantities frozen on beach, delicious to eat... great scarcity of bread ... soldiers guarded the carts carrying it to the garrison.

15th November 1791. Each evening - card playing at the club (the King's Arms) quite shocked because Mr. Martin (the Vicar) and church-wardens played until 12 o'clock at night ... Alexander Makenzie, the new Curate, offended many of the congregation by being too outspoken about vice in the village ...

July 2nd 1792. The Minister and friends got drunk at the feast ... The villagers got drunk at the loading of the hoy with copperas, in fact 12 out of the 16 houses in the village were drunk ...

"1793. Dispute over the 'Vicars perks', bottle of wine missing ..."

"1794. Mr Shrubsole preached a very fine sermon at Sheerness ..."

Stephen Rouse records the Nore Mutiny, he writes that on May 14th 1797, he was on the cliffs at Minster watching the revolt between the sailors. And in June ... "Mutiny crushed, prisoners brought ashore ... 'the Light Horse' went to guard Richard Parker on his way to Sheerness to be tried for treason".

On June 30th 1797. Stephen Rouse saw Parker hanged on H.M.S. Sandwich, and in July he saw sailors hanged on H.M.S. Leopard. In the following days he witnessed the hanging of four men on the Sandwich at the 'Black Stakes', altogether he watched fourteen executions and many whippings.

November 19th 1798 he "buried a man who died from being horse-whipped by the parish beadle."

"1798. Visited Harty to watch the Hoy races between Whitstable and Sheppey, there was a fair and two bands came from Sheerness ..."

"July 1st 1801. Press gang ... took ploughman ... farmworkers and many hid in the fields and did damage to the corn ..."

"August 22nd 1805. Attended the hanging of a man for sheep stealing ... A woman dressed in white did penance in the church ..."

"October 1805. On this day I stood upon the hill and watched H.M.S. Victory sail into Sheerness with Nelsons body aboard ..."

With this entry we leave Stephen Rouse and his diary. He died in the year 1814 aged 88 years, and we can feel gratitude to this energetic and worthy man of Minster; who by his punctiliousness and attention to small details has left behind this record of life in Minster in the turbulent days of the 18th century.

Many of the mutineers of the Nore Mutiny were buried in the annexe cemetery at Minster and at Eastchurch. In the old burial ground behind the hospital was a tombstone with this startling inscription O Earth cover not my blood, Sacred to the memory of a man unknown, who was found murdered on the morning of April 22nd, 1841, near Scrapsgate in this parish, by his head being nearly severed from his body.

A reward of one hundred guineas was offered on "conviction of the perpetrators of this horrid act", but they remained undiscovered.

Rumour had it, that this man surprised a party of smugglers, who themselves arranged for this impressive memorial.

One of the oldest burials recorded in the church register is interesting historically, it reads ... December 1591, Signor Geronino, a Spainyarde, prisoner to Sir Edward Hoby, taken in the fight with the Spanish Fleet in 1588, was buried this Vth day.

In the year 1809 a Major Hobson became the lay Rector of Minster. He was a far seeing man and believed that children should be taught, so he built a school in his own church, in the upper part of the north east chancel, and it was here that Stephen Rouse taught his pupils. When the Rector died he left a sum of money to pay the school fees of certain children chosen by the Vicar and Wardens.

When free education became law, this money was used for prizes to be given to regular scholars who made no less than 300 attendances and were nine years old.

In 1876 the school was built, two years later in 1878, Queen Victoria ordered the renovation of all parish churches. Minster Church was once again in a sadly ruinous condition, and extensive repair work was due. The old schoolroom was removed and the two old subscriptive pews were removed to the choir stalls. One of these pews belonged to the Vicar, the other to parsonage Farm; written documents giving permission to move them were displayed with the plans for the alterations. At this time the South porch was rebuilt also.

The only part of the historical monastic building which remains is the Abbey Gate house and part of the ancient wall, the gate house was a residence for many years and during the late 1800s it was used as a tenement for farmworkers on the Abbey Farm, it then remained unoccupied and in a ruinous state for a long time.

Charles Dickens often visited his friend, Captain Johns, who lived at

Prospect Place on Minster Hill. The young daughter of Mr Burford, the Churchwarden, was frequently carried pick-a-back through the church-yard by the great writer, and it is believed that the closing chapters of 'The Old Curiosity Shop' were inspired by the ancient church; the description fits precisely.

In 1889 the old workhouse was burned down on the evening of Thursday March 7th. The fire broke out a little before six, and as a very strong South wind was blowing, it was soon reduced to ashes. The village has much to be thankful for; had the wind been from the west, the whole of the cottages between the workhouse and the Rectory would have probably been burnt; as it was, if the next building, the chapel, had been of wood instead of brick, there is little doubt that the fire would have spread. Happily only one family was occupying the building, the children being got out just in time, some of them being in bed. Minster, the Mother parish of the Island, was formed into a separate Civil parish under the local Government Act of 1894.

In 1901 the Lord of the Manor was Mr. A. W. Howe Esq: the area of the Parish (without Sheerness) was 7,076 acres, assessable value £6,095. the population (1891) was 1,619 persons, the school, with accommodation for 200 pupils, had 174 with an average attendance of 146. The directory for 1901 gives the names of some of the houses, Borstall Hall Farm (Mr. C. Ingleton), East End Lane, (Oak Lane) Pigtail Gardens 3, East End farm, Cliff Cottage, Rose Cottage, Royal Oak Inn, Holly Bush Hall (Mr. T. Beal), Old Coastguard Station. Danedale Lodge (Dr. Julius Caeser). Chapel Street, Sons of Sheppey, Babies School. The forge.

In 1928. Mr Ramuz, who owned the Gate-House, offered it to the Archbishop of Canterbury, to be used for the parishioners as a library and museum. The Parochial Church Council issued an appeal for £1,000 to completely restore it to its former dignity, the appeal was a success and the ancient building restored, the museum, however, did not materialise, and in 1967 the Ecclesiastical Commissioners offered it, and the footpath used by the local inhabitants, to the Council.

The cottage and premises adjoining were demolished and a car park made. Vandals did some damage to the fabric but the council have now repaired it and tidied the surrounds. Great vigilance is required to preserve this relic of bye gone days and the people of Minster are aware of the fact and will jealously guard their gate-house from further damage.

One of the ancient Manors of Minster, was Borstal Hall, it was the home of William Cromer, son-in-law of Lord Saye and Sele of Rushenden Manor. Both were involved in Jack Cade's rebellion, and both were beheaded, their property confiscated by the Crown. The original manor house was replaced by a Georgian mansion in the 18th century.

In the 1900s it came into the possession of Mr. Ramuz, who renamed it Gilbert Hall. It was totally destroyed by fire in 1949.

Another historical home in Minster is Norwood Manor, it was occupied by the de Northwoode family for 500 years. It was vested with all the other manors in Sheppey to 'General Purposes' by Oliver Cromwell, and thus another great name was lost to Minster.

Neats Court, which formed part of the dowry of Queen Henrietta Maria, suffered the same fate, as did Scocles, Kingsborough, Rushenden manor and others, Minster Church was robbed of its wealth, tombs were mutilated, and some were hastily buried, to be found centuries later. It is believed that the church plate was hidden from Cromwell, but it has never been found.

Not only were manors and churches despoiled during Oliver Cromwell's 'Protectorship' but all records were destroyed. The owners of the great houses, deprived of all their possessions, fled to France, were imprisoned in the Tower, or beheaded.

The invasion of the Dutch in 1667, finished what Oliver Cromwell started, the down-fall of Sheppey; for what few landowners remained, left the island.

Thus, over the years, with the growth of Queenborough and Sheerness, Minster, the Mother Parish of the island, gradually sank into a quiet sleep, and became the tranquil back water as we know it today, with only memories of its former greatness. Scarcely anything remains of its past history, except a pile of stones and a few names, and a story to tell our grandchildren; that they may be forever reminded of their glorious heritage.

3 THE ORIGINS OF MINSTER ABBEY

The very name of its Royal Foundress and Patron Saint carries us back to the days of Saxon Heptarchy. In her rude age, when life and property were of precarious tenure, when a Royal or noble widow became an object of desire to any unscrupulouse baron, their only security seemed to lie in consigning themselves to the protection of the Church, and dedicating themselves to the service of God. Out of this state of society arose the custom of religious endowment and self dedication.

Thus it came about that Ethelburga, the daughter of the Royal converts, Ethelbert and Bertha, made for herself a sanctury at Lyminge. Her example was followed by the three daughters of Annas, King of East Anglia; Ethelfrida and Wytburga founded monasteries at Ely and at Dereham in Norfolk; while Sexburga, upon the death of her husband, Ecombert, King of Kent and grandson to Ethelbert, devoted her widowhood and wealth by founding a monastery at Minster in Sheppey.

The date generally assigned to the dedication of this building was AD 675. Here Sexburga became the first Abbess; but four years later upon the death of her sister Ethelfreda, she took her place as Abbess of Ely. Her daughter Erminhilda became the next Abbess of Minster and upon the death of Sexburga in AD. 699 became Abbess of Ely also. Sexburga was canonised in AD 709.

The chosen site had great advantages; its high position made it conspicuous to every voyager on this great highway into England; it also commanded the Island itself, the lordship of which was in her hands.

It is interesting to trace the changes through which the name of this Island has passed. The fame of its pastorage is preserved in its old Saxon name of Schepeye (The island of Sheep), which in the Norman language was latinised into Scapeia - while the monastic writers, anxious not to lose the origin of the name called it Insula Ovium. But Sexburga's religious house gave it a new name, Monasterium Scapeiae; this in the twelfth century was abridged into Moynstre, and in a little time to Menstre, and eventually into its present form of Minster retaining in Sheppey to distinguish it from Minster in Thanet.

Here St. Sexburga planted her Abbey, and its Chapel, for her seventy seven nuns. In the course of time there rose up by its side a parish church, for the use of the outside inhabitants who would soon be drawn into its vincinity for the purpose of trade or security.

It would for many years have been the only Church in the Island.

In the process of time other daughter chapelries grew up, now seperate parish churches of Queenborough, Eastchurch, Warden and Leyesdown. The nomination of the priest first lay with the Abbess, and eventually the right was granted to the Abbot and Convent of St. Agustine's Canterbury; from whence came the two monks, one as chaplain and confessor for the Abbey, the other as Vicar of the parish church.

They lived in apartments in the eastern gable of the gatehouse adjoining.

For two hundred years the Abbey enjoyed a peaceful existence, when in the ninth century came the Danes, swooping down on the seaboard of Kent, making two attacks on the Abbey and desecrating it.

Again in the eleventh century it fell prey to the sacrilegeous band of the banished Earl Godwin, whose followers committed further devastation. Thus it came that William of Normandy in the latter part of the century found the Abbey almost empty, and transfered to it the sisters from Newington Abbey, who had lost their devoted Prioress, murdered in her bed.

After the Conquest the first mention of Menstre occurs in the reign of Henry I, when in 1130, Archbishop William Corboil, after having held the grand dedication of Canterbury Cathedral, rescued the Abbey Chapel from ruin, added to it the parish church, and rededicated it as the Minster Church of St. Mary and Sexburga.

The next benefactor was Sir Roger Northwoode, a descendent of Jordanus de Scapeia, and Lord of Sheppey. It was from a private history of this family, preserved among the Surrenden MSS., that we learn that Sir Roger, who died in the year 1286, had so great affection for the Minster which had fallen into ruin - that with no sparing bounty he relieved it from great poverty, therefore among the servants of God there (the Nuns) he was called the restorer of that house; and that he was buried before the alter at Menstre.

In the middle of the next century (1322) a sad event befell the Minster. It is vaguely alluded to in an entry in Archbishop Reynold's Register at Lambeth, where it is said that both Church and cemetary suffered pollution from bloodshed, and the Archbishop was entreated to grant a Faculty for holding a special Service of Reconcilliation there.

When we reflect that above twelve centuries have passed since Sexburga founded this Abbey - that the invasions of the Danes and of Earl Godwin, the legalized spoilation of the Tudor in the sixteenth century, and the fanatic destructiveness of the Puritan in the seventeenth, the ceaseless exposure to the elements on this exposed height, have all had their share in domolishing it - one can hardly hope to find a single vestige of the original building.

Yet, high up in the south wall of this Chapel, above the bays which separate it from the ajoining parish church, may still be seen the rude circular arches of the old Saxon clerestories composed of Roman tiles, springing from rough stone jambs; while on the outside of the north wall may be also detected traces of corresponding openings half a similar arch cut in two by a Perpendicular window.

Here, too, between the tower and the first buttress, at intervals of about six feet apart, are pieces of ancient pottery, which carry the mind back to a still earlier period. These are believed to be Roman flue tiles, of a hypocaust, belonging to a Roman balneum or bath, still retaining on their sides the traces of the old maker's marks. On a recent restoration of this building it was seen that these went through the wall, with a wider mouth inside, which unhappily the contractor has plastered over, thus robbing us of any clue to the possible or probable object of their insertion with such methodical regularity in this wall.

Yet the fact remains, and the regularity shows that it was no haphazard arrangement, but that it had an object, and a use.

Now, what was it? Could it not have been for an acoustic purpose? Bearing in mind that the Garth or garden of the Nunnery lay on the north side of the Chapel, still retaining the traditional name of The Nun's Walk, and the cloister ran under its wall (of which some traces may still be detected), is it an utterly ludicrous inference that these were used as sound conductors placed here for the benefit of the nuns, who, spending much of their time in their daily avocations of teaching or embroidery sitting here under the cloister, might the more easily hear, and in spirit join in, the services of the Chapel within?

Other marks too, of the presence of Roman buildings in this vicinity are to be found. Not only in the arch of the clerestory and in the flue tiles, but in the entire length of the north wall, especially near its; eastern end, are traces of Roman bricks inserted promiscuously, which have happily escaped the contractors' plaster, and show that Roman buildings must at one time have stood in this neighbourhood, from which the Saxon and subsequent builders freely helped themselves.

It is at the east end of this Chapel where (under a lofty early English arch, spanned by a rood screen of three or four mullioned tracery, once stood the Sanctuary) we find what may be called the chief enigma of the building. Here the masonry of the north wall, both inside and out, differs from the more western portions of the Chapel, and evidently belongs to a later period.

This Chapel must once have extended some distance beyond the present east wall, for the two-seated sedillia are now close to that wall, and leave no space for piscina and credence beyond; and the piscina, having been preserved, has been inserted into the east wall; where also have been introduced other portions of carved stonework, which most certainly were not here originally.

In the centre is a triplet of recessed niches, once surmounted by a richly decorated canopu, crocket and finial (now all chiselled away), the middle one more deeply recessed and containing the mutilated remains of an image; while on the outside have been built in three ogee-pointed arches of stone, sadly pulverised, which might have once formed parts of a row of decorated arches, or windows; and inside are the jambs and arch of a doorway inserted in the north corner.

This Chapel, too, appears to have been originally flat-roofed, for the east wall retains marks of the resting places of massive beams, while the outside distenctly shows more recent masonary in its upper portion.

Here we must digress a little from the details of the Church to trace the changes which came over the Manor of Shurland, with which the Abbey seems to have been so closely connected, and to mark how these changes materially affected the Chapel itself.

Sir Robert de Shurland, whose monument in the south wall of the Church will be dealt with later, left an only daughter, who married Sir William Cheyne of Patricksbourne, into whose family the Shurland estates then passed; and with their descendants they remained till the time of Henry VIII, when Sir Henry Cheyne sold the Manor to Sir Humphrey Gilbert, who again exchanged it to Elizabeth, who bestowed it on her kinsman Sir Edward Hoby.

In this transfer seems to have been included the right to a certain family mortuary chapel of the Cheyneys, for the demolition of which, and the removal of the tombs and coffins a licence was granted by Archbishop Grindal in 1581.

The question then arises, which Chapel was this and where did it stand? In different wills, and in inventory of the goods of the Monastery, take in 1536 (Henry VIII), mention was made of three chapels, one of St. Mary, another of St. Katherine, and a third of St. John Bapist.

The latter is expressly stated in the inventory as standing in the church-yard. Now local tradition seems inclined to place that of St. Katherine at the Chancel of the parish church; and at first sight this seems natural, as that of St. Mary might be expected to be in the Nunnery Chapel; but it must be borne in mind that the name of the Virgin does not seem to appear in connection with the building until Archbishop Corbeiul restored the then ruinous church, and united the name of the Virgin with that of Sexburga the real foundress. Prior to that time it had always been known as the Monastery of St. Sexburga.

On the other hand, the Chapel of St. Katherine is distinctly connected with the Cheyne family as their burial place. Sir William Cheyney in his will, dated 1441, expresses the wish to be buried in it, as being the place where his ancestors lie, and leaves a legacy for its repair.

The very wording of that will connects the Chapel with the Nunnery, within the Abbey of SS. Mary and Sexburga. His son, Sir Thomas Cheyney, expresses a similar wish, in 1559, and desires "a tombe to be made nygh to the place where my late wyfe Frydeswyth do lye in my chapel at Minster".

It is eveident that the Chapel which was removed by Sir Humphrey Gilbert under the licence from Archbishop Grindal lay at the east of the Nunnery Chapel, now the north aisle. Most unfortunately that licence only says a certain small chapel, giving no name, and describing it as being near or adjacent to the Church of Minster. The Abbey Chapel must have projected farther estward, as already noticed; and here, whether as part of, or detatched from, the Chapel, must have lain the family mausoleum of the Cheyneys.

It is not probable that, when this was sold to Sir Humphrey Gilbert (who as we know, pulled it down and sold the materials), the present east wall was run up, cutting short the once goodly chapel beyond, and that then, too, its miscellaneous fragments - the arches, the triple niche, the doorway (which probably had been the Priest's Doorway in the north wall, giving entrance to the chaplain from the Abbey grounds adjoining) - were built up as interesting relics on the inside, while the stone tracery archwork was inserted on the outside?

Such a suggestion certainly seems to find some support in the presence of Perpendicular tracery in ther window which appears in the north wall; this would probably have been an insertion of that period, and no doubt formed part of the changes then introduced here.

But there is another perplexing feature in this Church, the seven square recesses in the upper part of the east wall. But whether they were the resting places of beams supporting a flat roof, or a gallery for the use of the nuns, must, remain an open question.

Let us now turn to the Parish Church portion of this building.

When it was added there is no direct record. At what exact time, beside the Chapel, built for the private devotions and the services of the high-born sisterhood, rose the Church in which the poor might have the Gospel preached to them, is not known; probably not earlier than the beginning of the twelfth century, as already suggested.

The circular arch leading from the porch into the Church, which from the depth of its hood-moulding was clearly once an outer door, Norman in shape, but with finer and lighter shafts and dog-tooth ornament, points to the Transition Period which connected the Norman with the Early English style, and would belong to the time of Henry II (1154 - 1180).

It is possible that (as has been conjectured from traces which were discovered at the recent restoration of the foundations of a massive doorway in the middle of the western bay of the north aisle) it originally stood here as the entrance door into the Monastic Chapel, and was removed to its present site when Archbishop Corbeuil started on his great work of repair in the year 1130.

The lofty lancet windows, which must have ranged over three sides of the Church, certainly belong to that time. Of these one remains on the west gable, two others have been sacrificed to make room for a three-light Perpendicular; three remain on the south; a fourth having given way to a four-light square-headed late decorated one; while a graceful triplet, recently restored, adorns the east end. But of any earlier work, if such existed, not a vestige now remains in the Parish Church.

The next addition would apparently carry us over two centuries, when the decorated window in the south wall already mentioned, and the exquisitely graceful canopy of the Shurland tomb, were introduced.

The massively based tower, which stands at the west end of the Chapel, next demands notice. But before describing this, it should bo noted that the tower seems to replace two campaniles or belfries whic evidently existed here; one belonging to the Abbey Chapel, and the other to the Parish Church; both of which must have fallen into disrepair towards the end of the fifteenth century, as we learn from Wills in the Archdeacon's Court at Canterbury, in which are frequent bequests for their repair.

Among others is that of one Peter Cleve, who died in 1479, leaving among other legacies a sum of money for the repair of the Chapel of St. John Baptist, and two of £40 each, one for the campanile on the Priory side, and the other for that on the side of the Parish Church.

This may account for the two spiral stairs, one on either side of the tower at its junction with the nave; and may help to assign the date for the addition of the tower to the Transition Period, as the character of the building suggests.

The loftiness of the arch between it and the Chapel would point to the latter years of the Decorated, while the capitals and bases indicate the incoming of the Perpendicular; and the features of the latter are still more pronounced in the square head, and the label, and shields in the spandrils, of the western doorway.

Then, too, would have been added the buttresses with their lollowed plinths along the face of the previously plinthless north wall. But the dark days for monasteries - for this Minster and its Chapel - were drawing near.

The time was at hand when their reputed wealth, and also their reputed abuses, were becoming nototious, and helping to accelerate their downfall; when their suppression, and the transfer of their ample and too often misused revenues, were to seal their doom, and to enrich needy and scrupulous courtiers.

That massive base, supported by double buttresses at each of the western angles, surmounted by a dwarf pent-house or capping tower of wood, tells of a design to erect a stately beacon tower, crowned, may be, by a loftier spire, to guide the seafarer up the Thames by day and night; but it now stands as an unfinished monument of the practical munificence of the monks of old, or rather the devoted sisters who had here made their home, and as one of the very many similar evidences of the rapacity of Henry VIII and his court.

Before leaving the fabric of the Church, it will be interesting to note some allusions made in several wills to side altars and images which once existed in the Church and the Chapel.

There were the High Altar, the Altar of the Virgin Mary, and also of St. Katherine; there were images of St. Mary le Pety, of the Holy Cross, and of St. James; these seem now impossibel to localise.

Besides the three-fold recesses already mentioned as now inserted in the east wall of the Chapel, there are also two recesses in the east wall of the Church, on on either side of the east window,

which no doubt were once filled with frescoes; that on the north side has been obliterated by plaster, while the one on the south still retains traces of a figure, and the letters Nich....lai, indicating that it was designed to represent St. Nicholas, the Patron Saint of sailors.

Now we notice that at about twelve feet from the floor in the north wall of this Chancel two very elegant lancet shaped recesses, which some think may have been openings through which the nuns could view the Host in the Chancel of St Mary; but as there is no trace of any opening extending through the wall, it is more probable that they were merely niches, either for images or for lights.

The Monuments.

The architectural features of this Church possess few points of interest in comparison with those of the Monuments. These are alive with local history.

They tell us of the successive families of note which from the thirteenth to the sixteenth centuries were Lords of Sheppey; for each family has its representative here - Shurland, Northwoode,Cheyney.

Taking them in chronological order, the one that claims priority in point of time, and also of artistic and historic interest, is that in the south wall of the Chancel. Here lies a knight in his shirt of mail, over which falls his loose surcoat, his head pillowed on his heaume or casque, his left hand still retaining its grip of the thong of his tapering convex shield, on which he is lying; his gauntleted right hand (the arm broken away) resting on the hilt of his sword, as though he had just dropped it into its scabbard; his bannered lance laid down beside him, yet eithin easy grasp; his legs crossed Crusader-wise; while close at his feet (not under them, as in the case of a lion or a dog) sleeps his boy page, his head resting on his arm bent under him, ready to spring up at the slightest touch to attend his lord's behest.

The whole group is a perfect study; the knight has fought his fight, and has laid him down to rest.

Who is this noble knight? The horse's head in the background, rising up as it were out of the water, the waves almost touching his nostrils, provides the clue, and tells its tale.

Towards the end of the thirteenth century the Manor of Shurland was held by one Sir Robert of that ilk, who had taken part in the Crusade of 1271, under Prince Edward (afterwards King Edward I) by whom also he was created Knight - Banneret for gallantry at the Siege of Carlaverock, and rose to high honours.

Now sundry traditions connect him with a strange scene and a daring exploit on a favourite horse, which saved his life by swimming to shore, where an old woman, seeing him landing after his perilous adventure, in comment on his rashness, warned him that that horse, would aome day be the death of him. This had so deep an effect on his superstitious mind that to render the hag's prediction impossible he drew his sword and killed the horse on the spot.

Some years after, seeing the skeleton lying on the shore, he gave the head a contemptuous kick, and in so doing bruised his foot, of which injury he eventually died, thus unconsciously fulfilling the prediction.

To perpetuate the tradition a horse's head was placed on the tomb, and also on the vane of the Church spire; this explains why the Minster is sometimes called "The Horse Church".

But the interest of this monument does not rest here. The figure lies on a base, and is covered by a canopy, of a much later date than that of Robert de Shurland's death. The elaborate panelling on the face of the tomb, and the bold yet very graceful tracery of the rich Decorated work above it, point to more than half a century after.

Grand and beautiful it must have been when its heavily crocketed (but now broken) arch and massive finial rose up to the very roof, from imposts still retaining in wonderful perfection and sharpness the head of a veiled nun on one side, and on the other that of a man whose thick rolling curls suggests the times of Edward III, or Richard II.

It has been thought that this tomb was probably designed for some very different effigy, it may have been for some high-born and distinguished Prioress, whose memory the sisters of the Priory desired to honour. But it would seem that for some now unknown cause the original design was never carried out, and the tomb remained unoccupied, and that when the Chapel or mausoleum (whether it was that of St. Katherine or of St. John the Baptist) was demolished, the figure of this grand old knight was found there among the ancestors of the Cheyneys; and because it exactly fitted the vacant space under the canopy, was placed there.

We have it on record that other tombs (that for instance of Sir Thomas Cheyney) wre originally in that Chapel, and were removed into the body of the Church, where they at present stand; and this of Sir Robert de Shurland might have been rescued in the same manner.

Next in point of time are the two brasses which lie in the centre of the Chancel, on either side of the lectern. These, now on seperate slabs, were until lately side by side on a large block of Betherden marble (now hidden under the choir stalls,) though no doubt they originally rested each on its own altar tomb.

Their general character - the clean cut outline of the figure inlaid in a corresponding indented matrix, instead of forming part of a large oblong unbroken plate, including effigy, canopy, shields, and probably inscription-scroll, as is customary with foreign brasses - would seem at first sight to infer that they were English work; but a closer examination of the details - the finer lines, with the intervening spaces chiselled out, instead of the deep bold lines with which an English graver would produce the shading of the figures - indicate in both brasses a French or Flemish hand, and such they are pronounced by experts to be; an opinion further confirmed by the style of dress of the female figure.

The question then arises, whom are they supposed to represent? Weever, in 1631 surmised that they were of Sir Roger de Northwoode and his wife Bona Fitz-Bernard, but the armour refutes the theory that it was meant to represent a man who lived in the thirteenth century. The light bascinet, instead of the heavier heaume or helmet, the haubert of banded ring--mail, in the place of the simple chain armour, associated with the Crusader times, the plated shoulder-piece and elbow-piece, too - all mark the transition period of the earlier years of the fourteenth century, and combine to strengthen the claim of another member of the Northwoode family,Sir John, the son of Sir Roger, who was even more distinguised in the annals of the country; who was also created a Knight - Banneret, and had by marriage allied himself with one of the most powerful and influential of Kentish families, the Badlesmeres.

Assuming then that these brasses represent Sir John Northwoode and his wife Joan (de Badlesmere) we are able to fix the date of their deaths. Sir John died in May 1319, and she in the following June; she was thus spared the sorrow of knowing that her father, Bartholomew, (Lord Badlesmere), three years after, paid the penalty of his refusal to admit Queen Isabella into Leeds Castle, of which he had been appointed Custodian by Edward II.

Now of the figures themselves, each was composed of two pieces; that of the lady has retained its original form; but the lower portion of the knight's brass has undergone more than one change.

Until a few years ago there lay, as a drawing in Stothard's Monumental Effigies shews, a broad space between the middle of the shield and the grotesquely misshapen legs, this has been accounted for by the supposition that it was at one time proposed to lay the two figures on one stone; but the disparity of the height was met by applying the Procrustean process, and cutting away enough from the middle of the body to reduce the height, and to make it correspond with the female figure, which made the addition of the lower limbs the more ludicrous.

The research of the late Dr. Maitland, while librarian at Lambeth, brought to light an interesting entry in the Lambeth Registers, which enables us to conjecture the date of this strange suffix. In the year 1511 the Churchwardens of Minster made a presentation to the Archbishop (Warham) at his Visitation to this effect, that wheare a long tyme ago in the Chapel a knight and his lady were buryed, the pictures upon them were sore worn and broken, and they requested permission to remove them.

But the Archbishop's Commissary admonished them to implore his Grace for permission that they might be repaired. It is most probable that the addition was then made; and that (utilizing as a palimpsest a portion of another brass, on which was engraved the drapery of a female figure) on the back of it was designed by some iliterate local workman what he fancied might have been the form of the crossed legged Crusader knight.

The lapse of 200 years, and the ignorance of the engraver, would easily account for the gross incongruity.

The next and the last step in the metamorphosis of the Northwode knight took place a few years ago, when the Church was being restored.

A member of that family supplied the gaping interval between the upper part of the figure and the grotesque legs, by introducing a third peice, on which the remainder of the shield and the armour were engraved, with far more harmonious effect.

The Northwode interest in Minster would seem to have continued for some generations. The eldest son of this Sir John, also a Sir John, was buried here; again, the first wife of his eldest son, a Sir Roger, and their son, a Sir John too, who died in 1379, found burial here.

The next monument to be noticed is that standing under the eastern bay of the colonnade which separates the Parish Church from the Abbey Chapel, and forms the most conspicuous monument in the church.

On a massive tomb of Bethersden marble, with its sides and ends richly ornamented with sixteen escutcheons proclaiming the proud alliances of the Cheyney family, lies an alabaster figure of a knight in full court costume of the latter years of the sixteenth century, with the badge of the Garter lying on his breast, and the ribbon at his knee.

It has been already said that on the death of Sir Robert de Shurland, the marriage of his only child Margaret with Sir William de Cheyney carried the Manor of Sheppey to the Cheyneys of Patricksbourne; and although the family pride and interest in the Sheppey estates flagged somewhat under the Cheyneys, yet it is clear that they looked to Minster as their ancestral burial place.

This monument, as the now partially effaced inscriptions running round the verge still shews, was in memory of Sir Thomas Cheyney, who had been Knight of ther Garter, Lord Warden of the Cinque Ports, Constable of Dover Castle, Treasurer of the Household to Henry VIII, and Edward VI., and Privy Councillor under Mary and Elizabeth.

In spite of all his honours, his heart, as shewn by his will, reverted to the old family home, and like his ancestor Sir William, who had died in 1441, he left the following record of his wish:

I will (he said) that my bodye be buryed in the Minster in the Isle of Sheppey,in a chapel there, wheare my late wyfe Dame Frydeswith and divers of myne ancestors are buryed.

This wish was carried out in 1559; but his son, Sir Henry; (created by Elizabeth in 1572 Lord Henry Cheyney of Tuddington), parted with the Minster estates to Sir Humphrey Gilbert, who pulled down and sold the materials of what had been the family chapel of the Cheyneys; the one redeeming act in this sad transaction being that, though Lord Cheyney sold to a stranger the chapel his father had so loved,he had the grace to solicit from the Archbishop of Canterbury a licence to remove his father's tomb, and the remains of other ancestors, and placed the tombs in the body of the church, where they now stand, having happily suffered very little disfigurement or mutilation.

There lies the old knight in all the grandeur of his official robes, his hands clasped, his head resting on a pillow richly diapered, and supported by angels; the most striking if not the most interesting monument in the Church of a man more than once described as a spriteful gentleman.

Here is another monument, which in point of time takes procedence over Sir Thomas Cheyne, in a far more lowly position, lying on the ground, with no raised altar tomb, no sculptured recess, to give it dignity; with no inscription, nor any heraldic device by which it might be identified, the only clue to its probable date being the armour, a plated breast-plate and tuilles, without a trace of a coat of mail either above or below; this would indicate the early part of the fifteenth century.

Its history, at least as much of it as is known, is strange.

It was found burried in the churchyard, in the year 1833, and here it lies in a vacant space against the north wall of the chapel; a knightly figure of Purbeck marble, on a coped slab; the face and upper part of the body in fair preservation, but feet and projecting portions of the thighs roughly chiselled away and sadly mutilated.

There is no trace of sword or dagger; the bare head rests on a pillow supported by two angels. The gauntleted hands are raised as in prayer, and here we meet with the most striking, it may be said unique, feature of the monument; between the tips of the fingers is a very small oval-shaped concave plate containing a very diminutive figure of a man (probably meant to represent has soul); it is this figure which gives the archaeological interest to the monument.

Why he was so mutilated - why he was buried in the churchyard - why so long left there uncared for and perhaps unknown - must now ever remain a mystery; as also - who he was.

This can only be conjectured by supposing that he belonged either to the Northwodes or the Cheyneys; one who died in the earlier half of the fifteenth century. If a Northwode, it may have been the John Northwode who died in 1416; or if a Cheyney, probably Sir William, whose death is recorded in 1441.

There remains yet another monument to be described. Under a plain arched recess in the north wall of this Chapel we see a tomb, with its front and the back of the recess composed of slabs of Bethersden marble richly diapered and panelled, and belonging to the fifteenth century, and on it the alabaster figure of a knight in full armour, the chain shirt appearing at the throat above the plated cuirass, the head resting on a pillow supported by angels; on his breast lies an Order, attached to a narrow ribbon embossed with alternate small roses and stars; the Order itself so worn and effaced that it is difficult to identify it with any known Order. More interesting than this, he is wearing a Yorkist collar of York roses alternating with sunbursts. The inscription which ran along the top of the tomb has long since been torn off, but the identity of the Knight is believed to be that of Hugh, Lord de Badesmere, a Yorkist knight killed in the Wars of the Roses.

Moving from the church and its monuments, let us glance at what remains of the Nunnery itself. Of its component parts all must now be conjecture. The gateway alone remains to bear silent witness to its former grandeur.

We may, however, reasonably imagine that a religious house which had for its first and second Prioresses members of the Royal house and in their successors ladies of high and often noble birth, would have every portion of its entourage complete.

The inventory taken at the time of the dissolution, gives some idea of its extent and self-sufficiency. There were the apartments of My Lady Prioress, Alica Crane; of Dame Ursula Gosborne? (Gisborne), who was called the sub-prioress; those of Dames Agnes Browne, Margaret ... locks, Dorothy Toplyve, Anne Loveden, Elizabeth Stradlynge, Anne Clifford, and Margaret Ryvers.

There are listed the greate chamber in the Dorter...the Frater...the Hall...the parlours...the greate bathe...the nether kechyn...the upper kechyn...the store howse...the chese howse...the bake howse...the brewe howse and the chamber over the Gate Howse, called the Confessors Chamber. There were then nearly forty rooms, and the Gate House is all that is left.

There would also have been the refectory, chapter-house, and garth, and cloisters, as well as the Chapel, all enclosed within a range of high walls.

All this, except the gatehouse, is gone; nor does a trace remain unless it be the line of a high-pitched roof on the west wall, where probably stood the spacious refectory.

The Gate House has been altered over the years; it was built at the same time as the Parish Church, in 1130, and after the suppression was used as a residence, the last notable occupant being Sir Humphrey Gilbert. In the ninteenth century it was utilized into tenements for the families of farm-labourers, and during the earlier years of this century the Rev Bramstone restored the Gate-House, opening up the great archway once again.

In Minster, as in the Benedictine Monastries generally, the discipline of the house was under Episcopal jurisdiction: while the election of the Prioress lay with the sub-prioress and the nuns,it required the preliminary sanction and subsequent confirmation of the Archbishop.

This is evident from an entry in the Lambeth Register, where Archbishop Stafford issues a licence to the sub-prioress and the convent to proceed to the election of a prioress on the death of the last Prioress. The internal discipline, too, of the house came under the control of the Primate.

In the same Registers we have glimpses of the life these nuns were accustomed to lead; and they are not always favourable pictures.

More than once it became necessary for the Archbishops to interfere, and sometimes to adminster warnings and even rebukes and threats. Archbishop Peckham in 1286 had to condemn the latitude which (as he had heard) allowed mulieres seculares (women who were not under the vow) to come inside the walls, and threatens them severely unless they mend their ways.

Ten years later Archbishop Winchelsea held a personal visitation, and found other grounds of complaint; he had heard that in refectory and dormitory, in cloister, and even in choir, the rule of SILENCE was not observed; that the nuns are said to be garrulous and quarrelsome; and for such delinquencies he enjoins periods of solitary confinement in the cells, and warns them that if this disorder continues still more severe forms of punishment must be resorted to to maintain the good order of the house.

Of the successive Prioress it is now impossible to give a full and correct list, as the names occur incidentally in various records. For instance, we read that one Agnes (whose surname is not given) was Prioress in 1139; that Joanna de Cobham filled the post in the middle of the fourteenth century, and that on her death in 1368 she was succeeded by Isabella de Honyngton, who had professed only a few months before.

These two ladies no doubt belonged to the old Kentish families of Cobham and Honington. Then in 1511 Alice Rivers was Prioress; and she very probably belonged to the family of which Elizabeth, the Queen of Edward IV., was a member.

The last of the Prioresses was Alice Crane, who held office at the time of the suppression, when she was pensioned.

We cannot do better than close this brief account of the Minster Nunnery than by referring to a highly interesting M.SS. in the British Museum (Cottonian MSS., Faustina, B.vi.) where a list is given of the memorial days of five of the Prioresses; this unfortunately gives only their Christian names, and consequently we are not able to identify them, or to give the years in which they died.

The names occur in the following order:-

2 Id. Martii,ob. Johanna de Badlesmere, Priorissa de Menstre.

12 Kal. Maii, ob. Eustachina, Priorissa de Mentre.

4 Non.Octobris, ob. Agnes, ditto.

13 Kal. Octobris,ob. Ghristina, ditto.

11 Kal. Decembris, ob. Gunnors, ditto.

4 THE HISTORY OF QUEENBOROUGH

Origins

The sub-division of the whole of England into parishes was essentially the work of Theodore, Archbishop of Canterbury, A.D. 669-690. The limits of the Parish of Minster were about this time approximately determined. It occupied the entire western part of the Island, and included therefore what is now the Parish of Queenborough, which was not then in existance. A few fishermen's huts on the creek made a village called 'Binney' Or 'Byne'...'eye'...an island.

The rising ground upon which the village, then and the town at present is situated, stood out at high tide as an island in the flooded marsh; before the sea-wall was built, spring tides overflowed all the low ground.

Upon this high mound, the Danish Prince Hoestan built a powerful fort in A.D. 893, The village of Bynne belonged to the monastery of St. Sexburga. This desolate marsh is what King Edward III's Queen Phillippa of Hainault, found when she was driven ashore here after the Battle of Crecy in 1346.

Edward III cut off from the original parish of Minster, the liberty of Queenborough and virtually created the parish, although its existence was not formerly recognised until nearly one hundred years later.

All marsh, moor and woodland was in Saxon and early Norman times absolutely in the Sovereign's hands, the common law followed the plough.

The Church was originally accounted as a chapel of the Mother Church of Minster and belonged with it to the monastery.

Here then are the origins of the Borough, nothing but a collection of small huts and the ruins of a Saxon castle until the 14th. century, when King Edward III became its benefactor.

Realising its strategic position at the mouth of the Medway, he decided to build a strong castle for the defence of the kingdom

The Prioress and the monastery recieved considerable material advantages from Bynne; from the 'Patent Rolls' of Edward III's reign in 1362, we learn that the Prioress and convent of the Monastery of

'Sheepeye' were granted the right to dig two pits or pools in which the rainwaters descend and are recieved, to have and to hold to the same Prioress and Convent and their successors forever.

Special licence was given. That trenches be dug, for the rainwater to run into the pits, and all the water could be drawn out at every time of the year and taken there from, by ships or boats, carts, horses, or other sumages whatsoever to the Priory, and that their successors, or men and servants may have free ingress and egress to the said place of Bynne by the middle of that same place with carts and horses, and all other animals, by the causeway which goes to the castle, and by all ways and paths from Menstre to Bynne, to drive their animals there to water.

Thus it can be seen, that provision was made for the Monastery and people of Minster to obtain their water from the pits or reservoirs in the marshes, also all fish and sea-food found in these pits belong to the Prioress.

In the year 1344, Edward III granted the right to hold a fair in the Island on Palm Monday, this continued annually until the last century. In 1361, the King commanded a new castle to be built where the ancient remains stood, the village was now called Minster Marshes.

The castle was designed by the King's architect, William de Wyckham, Bishop of Winchester, and built under the supervision of John Gibbon, ancestor of Edward Gibbon, the celebrated historian. The Gibbon family resided at Rushenden Manor for generations, being descended from the Lords Saye and Sele and the Cromers of Borstal Hall.

The castle consisted of one range of twelve rooms below stairs and about forty rooms from the first storey upwards, being circular and built of stone, with six towers and out-offices, the roof being covered with lead. Within the circumference of the castle was one small round court paved with stone; in the centre one large well which is still in use. Outside the castle a court surrounded it and the whole building was encompassed with a great stone wall and moat, the whole occupying some three acres.

So the castle was built, for the strength of Ye Realm and for the refuge of the inhabitants of the Island.

Leyland, writing of the castle says:-

A castle high and thundering shotte
at Queenborough is now plaste,
which keepeth safe the islanders
From every spoile and waste.

When the castle was completed in 1366, King Edward and his Queen Phillippa resided there. The King, in honour of his wife, converted the lands around, including Rushenden Manor, into a free borough, naming it Regina Burgia, or Queenborough as we know it to day, transforming Minster Marshes into a corporate town, making the villagers freemen and investing them with privileges and power to chose a Mayor and two baliffs yearly, the liberty of two weekly markets and two yearly fairs.

He appointed Sir John de Foxley as the first constable of Queenborough Castle; it was he who brought the olive wood wand from the Holy Land, which is still used as a staff of office today. Sir John died in 1377 and was succeeded by John of Gaunt, third son of Edward III.

Another great priviledge granted to Queenborough on May 10th 1368, was the right to Admiralty jurisdiction; such favours were only granted to places whose services were of value to the Crown. Queenborough and Rochester were the only places in Kent outside the cinque ports, thus honoured.

This privilege gave jurisdiction over all maritime matters except piracy. Queenborough also recieved a charter for its conversion into a wool staple for the export of wool.

The custom on wool, skins and leather, were formerly called hereditary customs of the Crown and were due only on the export of these three staple commodities. They were obliged to be brought to those ports where the 'King's Staple' was established,in order to be rated and exported.

This staple industry lasted for centuries at Queenborough. The only other place in Kent so honoured was Canterbury.

In latter years, (March 1527) Sir Thomas Cheyne had licence to export 500 bales of wool from his Sheppey estates.

In the year 1375 the King again held court at Queenborough and made serveral regulations for the better government of the Admiralty.

King Edward III, died on June 27th, in the fiftieth year of his reign. His son Edward the Black Prince had died the previous year, leaving his wife Joan, The Fair Maid of Kent, and his only son Richard, aged 10 years, to succeed to the throne.

John of Gaunt, his uncle, resigned his position as Constable of Queenborough Castle to become his guardian.

Later during his reign Richard II ordered coastal defences to be carried out and a watch and guard beacon was erected and men-at-arms and mounted hobeliers on small horses patrolled the coast; it is from the word hobelier that we get Hobby-Horse.

John of Gaunt quarreled with the King, and in the year 1398, his son Henry Bolinbroke also quarreled with Richard and was banished from the kingdom. Upon the death of John of Gaunt Henry returned and declared his intention of seizing the throne. Richard was taken prisoner and died shortly afterwards leaving no issue.

Henry Bolinbroke was crowned Henry IV. He made a long stay at Queenborough in the year 1406, to avoid a plague which had broken out in London. During his stay he ordered a better road to be made from Tremod Ferry to Sochelles, and granted the right to collect tolls for three years for the maintenence thereof.

The charge being:-

1d for every strange horseman, in or out of the Island.

1/2d for every footman, 1d for every loaded horse and 1/2d for every horse not laden.

Henry V was now on the throne. He appointed Gilbert de Umfeville as Constable of Queenborough Castle. This King spent most of his reign fighting in France, his son succeeded him when only one year old. During the reign of Henry VI in 1430, Jack Cade's rebellion broke out. The Duke of Buckingham, Constable of Queenborough, was ordered to quell the rebellion, he was taken prisoner and be-headed as were the Lord Saye and Sele of Rushenden Manor and William Crowmer of Borstal Hall, Sheriff of the County; their heads were stuck on poles and paraded through the streets of London.

Jack Cade, with a band of followers, came to Queenborough and attacked the castle but it was successfully defended by Sir Roger Chamberlayne. It is interesting to note the names of some of the rebels:- John Cheyne of Eastchurch; Will Baker, baker; John Lymond of Minster; John Cokeram, the Mayor of the new town of Queenborough, merchant; John Swaleman of Queenborough, yeoman; Will Britte; Will Canon; Galfrus Benet; John Britte; Alarus Jacob, Robt Sunster, and John Willys, who were all described as mariners. John Cade was captured and hanged, drawn and quartered for his uprisings.

On May 25th. 1455, The War of the Roses broke out and men of Sheppey fought in this long campaign.

In 1461, John de Northwoode was appointed Constable of Queenborough Castle , he resigned in favour of George Plantagenent, Duke of Clarence in 1465, who recieved the governorship of Sheppey.

Edward IV. died in 1483, leaving two small sons, Edward and Richard. Duke of York, their uncle, Richard, Duke of Gloucester, claimed protectorship and sent the children to the Tower of London for safe keeping, they died in mysterious circumstances.

Richard usurped the throne becoming King Richard III; during his reign we find an entry among the Harleian Manuscripts (No. 433) for a warrant of timber to be delivered to Christopher Colyns, for certain reparations at the castle of Queenborough.

In the same book is a commission empowering him to take masons, stores, etc. neccessary for works on the said castle.

It is evident therefore, that the castle was extensively repaired. Richard was unpopular and Henry Tudor, next in succession, came home from exile and contested the Crown.

At the battle of Bosworth Field in 1485. Richard was killed and Henry became King Henry VII. He was succeeded by his son Henry VIII. in 1509. The reign of this King brought an end to the monasteries, among them, Minster Abbey, all the lands and property, farms, windmill, and the monastery buildings were sold to Sir Thamas Cheyne for the sum of £198.

During the reign of Henry VIII, Queenborough Castle was again repaired. In the year 1554. Sir Thomas Wyatt led the Men of Kent in a Protestant rising against Queen Mary who inherited the throne upon the death of her brother Edward VI in 1553.

Wyatt was beheaded on April 11th 1554 and his estates in Sheppey with those of William Cromer of Borstal Hall were given to Sir Thomas Cheyne.

Upon the death of Mary, Queen Elizabeth I. succeeded to the throne and the Golden Age for England began.

In the year 1571, the Queen conferred on the Royal Borough of Queenborough the privilege of returning two members of Parliament annually. The first two members were John Cobham and John Parker, Cobham was re-elected in the three years that followed and died in 1594.

According to a return made to the Queen in 1566. there were in Queenborough, twenty three houses, twelve boats and ships belonging to the town, from four tons to sixteen, a quay and a landing place.

In the year 1563, Queenborough provided eleven small ships to sail against the Spanish Armada.

The dredging of oysters was for centuries a principal industry of Queen-borough, along with the Wool Staple and a shipping port.

In 1597. a new industry was introduced, Mathias Falconer, a Flemming, dicovered iron pirites in great quantities on the beach at Minster, he used these for the manufacture of sulphate of iron and built a small factory at Queenborough.

It was the first recorded manufacture of chemicals in this country and became the foundation of the present day chemical works there.

In February 1585, Dr. William Parry. M.P. for Queenborough, was convicted of conspiring to murder the Queen and was executed in March of that year.

It is interesting to note two ordinances passed by the Corporation, the first in 1582 was:- That the Mayor's Court decide that it is expedient to have a ducking stool made in the towne for the punishment of scouldes and the unquiet. And in 1584, The same jury do present all the inhabitants of the towne for bowling and such unlawful games wherefore every man is amerced to pay 8d into the poor man's boxe. In 1661, under this bye-law Mr. Richard Nicholls was fined £5 for abusing the Mayor and under-valuing his authority.

In the year 1582, Queen Elizabeth was the guest of Sir Edward Hoby at Queenborough Castle, which was a scene of royal splendour. A description of the great dining hall is given by Mr. Johnson in his book 'Inter Plantariam Investigations':- he tells us that:-

He saw in this castle, a noble large dining room or hall, round the top of which were placed the arms of the nobility and gentry of Kent and in the middle, those of Queen Elizabeth, underneath which was written this verse:-

Lillies, the lions virgin breast explain
Then live a virgin, and a lion reign.
Pictures are pleasing, for the mind they shew;
And in the mind the Diety we view;
May she who God in life and Empire shews
To me the Eternal Diety disclose;
May Jesse's flower, and Judah's lion deign
Thy flowers and lions to protect, great Queen.
                                        A.D. 1593.

The annual fee for the Constable of Queenborough in Elizabeth's time was £29-2-6. per annum.

An amusing story is told about the 'Queen's Elephant', it appears that when visiting Queenborough, the Queen sent for the Mayor, and he, being in ordinary life a thatcher, hastily scrambled down from a roof, tearing his leathern breeches. Having no others he appeared before Her Majesty, who, being slightly displeased at his appearance, ordered her steward to send to Queenborough yearly, one pair of leather breeches or an equivalent in place of them for the Mayor.

After several years the breeches piled up and the Mayor sent word to the court asking for the equivalent in place of them.

This application was mis-read by a clerk, who thought it read 'the Elephant', he forthwith sent word that the elephant would shortly arrive. The Townspeople of Queenborough, puzzled as to what they were to do with an elephant, nevertheless built an enclosure for it (some say this is the small square on the waterfront and some say it was the space beneath the Guildhall), and waited expectantly for the elephant to arrive, however, someone at court obviously more wide awake than the clerk, asked why the good people of Queenborough wanted an elephant and the letter was brought to light and the equivalent in the form of 10/- annually was duly sent.

In July 1588, a Spanish General, Don Cerinimo, commander of a treasure ship in the great Spanish Armada, was captured by Sir Francis Drake and imprisoned in Queenborough Castle in the custody of Sir Edward Hoby. He died there and was interred at Minster.

Queen Elizabeth died on March 24th 1603, she bequeathed the Crown of England to James IV of Scotland.

Lord Hunsdon, Lord of the Manor of Kingsborough Sheppey, witnessed the death of the Queen and was dispatched post haste to Scotland as a special messenger to aquaint King James with the news of his accession to the Throne.

The King was crowned James I of England on July 25th 1603, Sir Phillip Herbert, a great favourite of the King, was created Baron Herbert of Shurland, Earl of Montgomery and Knight of the Garter, he was the last Constable of Queenborough Castle. Considerable land drainage was carried out during the reign of James I, he was succeeded by his son the ill fated Charles I on March 27th 1625.

King Charles was an autocratic monarch and had great ideas of the Divine Rights of King. His views met with public resentment. He contracted an unpopular marriage with Henrietta Maria, daughter of the King of France.

The estate of Neats Court, some 640 acres, was given to her by the King as part of her marriage dower.

Thus for a time she became Lady of the Manor of Neats Court Minster.

The King levied 'Ship-money' to build a stronger navy; subsequently civil war broke out and in 1649 the King was arrested and charged with treason. Two of his judges at the trial were Sir Michael Livesy of Parsonage Farm Eastchurch, and Augustine Garland of Tam's Farm Minster, both Members of Parliament for Queenborough.

They signed the death warrant and Charles I was executed in public in Whitehall on January 30th 1649.

This King gave Queenborough a new charter, and under this charter the town was governed until 1885, when Queen Victoria granted a new municipal charter.

Oliver Cromwell became Lord Protector of England, all manors were dismantled, church property confiscated, garrisons disbanded and Queenborough Castle was pulled down.

Cromwell passed an ordinance that the castle may be surveyed and sold to supply the necessities of State. The surveyors judged it not fit to be kept but demolished and that the materials were worth, besides the charge of dismantling. £1,792-12s-01/2d.

It was sold to a Mr. John Wilkinson, who pulled the whole of it down and removed the materials. The site of this castle afterwards remained in his possession until the Restoration of Charles II in 1660, when the inheritance of it return again to the Crown, where it has continued ever since.

Here is a copy of an agreement for the sale of part of Queenborough Castle, dated 1650:-

Know ye all men by these presents that I, Daniel Judd of London, merchant, have recieved and had certified by sealing hereof of Henry Seager of Quinburrowe in the County of Kent, manor of the same, the sum of thirty pounds of lawful money of England and is in full payment of and for that barne stable and coachhouse, with ate appurtenances, situated and being within the walls of Quinburrowe Castle aforesaid and late belonging to the same castle and of and for all and every the timbers, stone, brick, tyles and others, the materials thereunto belonging, and of and for all my whole rights title and interest of in and to the same premises and any part hereof, and the whole golg for me of ....by me recieved as aforesaid, I do freely aquit and discharge the said Henery Seager, his eyers, administrators and assignes and every of them for ever, by these presents sealed, with my seal dated the sixth day of December 1650.

Sealed and delivered)
in the presence of)   L.S.
Ralph Smith and)   Daniel Judd.
John Wright)

Most of the records of Queenborough Castle and the Manor Houses of Sheppey were destroyed by Oliver Cromwell, who after five years of oppressive rule died in 1658

John Taylor, The Water Poet, who made a 'Penniless Pilgrimage' into Scotland in 1639, and rode a-hunting in the Highlands when Englishmen Knew as little of them as Timbuctoo, also visited Queenborough in a very extraodinary manner.

Having constructed a boat made of brown paper and bladders, Taylor, in company with a congenial soul, a jolly vintner named Roger Bird, sailed from London on a Saturday, and, after many adventures and dangers, found themselves to their great joy at daylight on the following Monday morning close to Queenborough where they landed, and Taylor thus describes their reception in his poem:-

The Praise of Hempseed by John Taylor, The Water Poet.

But being come to Queenborough, and a land,
I took my fellow Roger by the hand,
And both of us ere we two steps did goe,
Gave thanks to God that had preserved us so;
Confessing that His mercy us protected,
When as we least deserved and less expected,
The Mayor of Quinborough in love affords,
To entertain us as we had been lords;
It is a yearly feast kept by the Mayor,
And thousand people thither doth repaire,
From townes and villages that's near about,
And t'was our luck to come in all this rout,
I'th'street, bread, beer and oysters is there set,
Which freely, friendly, shoot-free all do eat,
But Rodge and I were men of rank and note

> We to the Mayor gave our adventurous boat
> The which (to glorify that town of Kent.)
> He meant to hang up for a monument,
> He to his house invited us to dine,
> When we had cheer on cheer and wine on wine,
> And drunk our fill, and drunk, and drunk our fill,
> With welcome upon welcome, welcome still.

The poet goes on to say how the merry townsmen tore the boat into a thousand scraps and wore the pieces in their hats for relica, and the next day with thanks, left Queenborough and went back home on horseback all in post.

On the 29th May 1660, the exiled King Charles II returned to England. Sir Michael Livesey fled to Holland and Augustine Garland was brought to trial - he was found guilty and was ordered to be hanged, drawn and quartered; the King intervened, and Garland was imprisoned and later deported to Tangiers in 1664, where he was sold into slavery.

Charles II, recognising the helpless condition of Sheppey, ordered a new fortification and dockyard to be built and accompanied by his chief engineer, Sir Bernard de Gomme, Sir William Brockman and Samuel Pepys, Secretary of State, He visited Sheerness on August 18th, 1665, to lay out the plan.

The King with his brother James, Duke of York, made several visits to the Island to inspect the progress of the work, they stayed at Neats Court and Holme Place during their visits.

Charles II. took a great interest in Queenborough and it is believed that he gave four of the bells in the church to commemorate the conclusion of peace with the Dutch, the date on them is 1667. His Chief Secretary of State, Sir Joseph Williamson, gave the beautiful Communion plate to the church.

In the year 1666, Samuel Pepys made this entry in his diary, dated June 12th:- To Woolwich and Deptford, all the way down and up, reading 'The Mayor of Quinborow' a simple play.

I discovered that Thomas Middleton, Rembrancer of the City of London in the 16th century, a renowned dramatist and playwright, wrote a stage play entitled 'The Mayor of Quinborow'.

Middleton who was born in 1570 and died in 1627, wrote the play early in life, but it was not published until some years after his death, as this

extract from the show bill indicates:-
The Mayor of Quinborow.

A comedy, as it hath been often acted with much applause at Black Fryers, by his Majesty's servants, written by Thomas Middleton, London, printed by Henry Herringham; and are to be sold at his shop, at the sign of the Blew Anchor, in the lower walk of the New Exchange, 1661. 4. to.

In the play His Worship the Mayor, on greeting Hengist, in Sheppey says:-

> So I. The Mayor of Quinborow by name,
> With all my brethren, saving one that's lame,
> Are come as fast as fiery mill - horse gallops
> To greet thy grace, thy Queen, and her fair trollops,

On June 10th 1667, the Dutch invaded Sheppey, taking possession of the hulks and stores at Sheerness, and removing masts and goods to the value of £40,000. They received the submission of the Mayor and Corporation of Quenborough, who came across the marshes with a white flag and in order to prevent blood-shed surrendered the town.

The emissaries of the invading Dutch came to the Guildhall and the Dutch flag was hoisted above it. It became the only town in England to fly the flag of an invader since the time of William of Normandy.

As a result of the invasion the King restored and fortified the garrison and the City of London voted a sum of £10,000 for the cost of the fortification.

The dockyard was constructed by the Admiralty at this time also.

Upon the death of King Charles II in 1685, his brother James, Duke of York, succeeded him. He took a great interest in the Island and owned manors and estates here.

The reign of James II was a stormy one and with a revolution pending the King sent his Queen and infant son to France and prepared to follow them; he stayed at Neats Court with Sir Edward Hayles. In disguise, he went with three friends to Elmley to await the hoy in which he hoped to sail to France, the Faversham sailors had been warned to look out for any ship leaving Sheppey.

The ship called at Shellness to take on ballast and the Faversham men searched her. The King and his party were arrested, however, and escorted to London on December 11th 1688; afterwards he was allowed to abdicate in favour of his daughter, Mary and her husband William of Orange. The King set sail from Queenborough on Christmas eve, nevermore to see England again.

William died in 1702, and the Crown passed to Anne, the Act of Settlement established Protestant Hanoverian succession in England. Queen Anne reigned only 12 years, and was succeeded by her nephew King George I in the year 1714.

About nine years later, the want of fresh water was much felt in Sheerness and the dockyard. It appears that in September 1723, The Right Honourable the Navy Board, gave instructions to survey the old well of Queenborough Castle, a party of twelve officers went to carry out the task but found very little water so they lowered a man down, he reported that the well was steined 200 feet down with circular portland stone, which was, all entire and stood fair.

Preparations were made to bore deeper down and after three days of boring, water came up; in an hour the water was four feet deep. It continued to rise until in ten days there was 176 feet of water, the distance bored was 81 feet, the water proved excellent. good, soft, sweet and fine.

Mr. Bourne, the foreman of the 'yard', was taking a plan of the castle land, but Queenborough rights were then, as now, jealously guarded. The Mayor and three more of the 'Bench' forbade this measurement to be made, claiming the right to the castle well and all appertaining thereto, and demanded the key of the well, threatening if it were not given up, to break the well open.

The officers refused, and set a watch on the well, the officers claiming the King's right to the castle, land and well, the Corporation denying it. The Lords of the Treasury wrote a letter to the Corporation on the matter, but the Mayor stood his ground. Estimates were sent to the Navy Board of the cost of conveying the water from the castle well to the creek, so the Navy made another boring in the Mote Marsh at Sheerness and a well 152 feet deep was dug for the sum of £1,035.

Thus the ancient rights and privileges of the Borough were maintained in defence of the Navy Board and the King, but whether the Navy Board gave the famished people of Sheerness any of the water from the well is not stated.

The notion of allowing the 'Yard' people to bore and obtain water in a well that was a dry one, and then putting in a claim to the improved property, was a piece of smartness on the part of the Corporation of that time.

King George II, succeeded to the Throne in 1727, and 'Pocket Boroughs' were formed. During his reign, in the year 1732, the painter, Hogarth, and four friends made a hilarious journey by boat from London, and made a five days perigination of the Isle of Sheppey; the account of which was written by Mr. Forrest, the 'Historiographer' of the merry expedition.

Upon reaching Queenborough he describes the High Street thus:-

There is no sign of any trade, nor were many human creatures to be seen at first arrival. They found, to their sorrow that although Queenborough was a market town, yet they could not procure one piece of fresh meat of any sort, nor poultry or fish. They however, got a wooden chair and placed Hogarth in it in the street, where he made drawing, and gathered a great many people to see his performance.

They visited the church and found nothing there worthy of notice, but they had a conference with the grave-digger who informed them that the Mayor was a Custom House Officer and the parson a 'sad dog'. Hogarth's party would have had another laugh if they had known that the Mayor, when not engaged in official duties followed his humble occupation of a thatcher; and if they had known the then incumbent's stipend was only £52 per annum, with a right of grazing worth about £7 more, they might have said that Queenborough people could not expect a 'very merry dog' for so little money.

In the year 1767, during the reign of George III, an act was passed, for the better and more effectual maintainence and relief of the poor of the Borough and Parish of Queenborough. A workhouse had been built in 1761, up to this date a house had been hired for the poor; the whole cost of building the new workhouse amounted to £150. The poor rate at this time was 1/- in the pound and the Church rate was the same.

Lord Nelson will forever be associated with Queenborough. After joining the Royal Navy, he was transferred to the Triumph guardship in the Thames estuary. He gained his knowlege of seamanship while sailing in these waters.

In 1783, he was appointed lieutenant on the Boreas at Sheerness and later given command of the Agamemnon on July 27th 1801. His duty was to organise the defence of the Thames and Medway against the threatened invasion by Napoleon.

Nelson would have often been seen in the High Street with Troubridge and Howe. He worshipped at Queenborough church and the house he occupied with Lady Hamilton stands on the west side of the church.

In 1790, an election took place at Queenborough. The candidates were Richard Hopkins Esq. Gibbs Crawford Esq. and Commodore Parker, R.N. The election was carried on for nine days and open house was kept for nine days and nights.

It would appear that the jolly freemen must have lived like fighting cocks and had a good time while the revelry of an election lasted; if we judge by the amount of refreshments disposed of at only one of several open houses:- The George, Queenborough, for this tavern bill amounted to the sum of £425-19-9.

On May 22nd 1797, the Mutiny at the Nore caused great consternation at Queenborough and Sheerness, but it was quelled by the Admirallty and on June 29th, Richard Parker, the self styled 'Port Admiral', was tried for treason as leader of the mutiny and hanged at the yard-arm of H.M.S. Sandwich.

In 1798, the town consisted of one main wide street, the houses of which were neat and mostly well built, numbering 120, the market house was a small ancient building in the middle of the street with a room over it.

The Court Hall was the upper part of a mean plastered dwelling house close to the churchyard. So wrote Hasted, the historian, and he adds, that not withstanding such an increase, both of houses and inhabitants, it was in his time (1798) a poor fishing town, consisting of ale house keepers, fishermen and oyster dredgers.

The principal source of wealth in those days seemed to be in the election of Members of Parliament which secured many lucrative places in the ordnance and other branches of government.

In fact for many years the Board of Ordnance nominated the members for the borough and the entire control of property and expenditure of the corporation ultimately fell into the hands of seven persons, the Mayor, four Jurats, and two Bayliffs who elected each other as they thought proper.

The Mayor was elected by those persons writing the name of their choice on a piece of paper which was folded up and given into the hands of the town clerk, whose office had become almost hereditary.

The town clerk then went home, and opening the papers announced the result of the elections by sending the Serjeant-at-Mace with a goose to the house of the person who had a majority of votes.

The Mayors were generally re-elected for considerable periods, one held office for twenty years; and as he was ex-officio returning officer for the Borough, this practice was decidedly illegal.

In 1803, the threat of another invasion by Napoleon Buonaparte caused great panic, and on July 6th a bill was hurriedly passed to form an army reserve for home defence, all men between the age of 18 and 45 were liable for the call up, and all single men from 17 to 30 to be armed and trained.

Queenborough was ordered to supply it's quota of men. Many of them paid the overseer of the parish one guinea to be exempted from serving, substitutes had to be found and bounty money paid. To do this a rate of sixpence in the pond was levied on every inhabitant to enable, to establish and maintain militia for the defence of the realm. This tax rate continued throughout the Peninsular War and was only withdrawn after the fall of Napoleon in 1815.

On October 21st 1805, Lord Nelson was killed at the battle of Trafalgar and his body was brought back to Sheerness on H.M.S. Victory. According to records of 1828, we learn that the Mayor of Queenborough was not above performing the offices of both judge and executioner, as his predecessors in the Mayoralty had done before him.

The general punishment for petty offences in Queenborough was a flogging; and the Mayors after passing sentences ex-officio would descend from the judgement seat, and with their own hands apply the lash. 'Men-of-Wars' men from the dockyard used to be very fond of larking excursions in the neighbouring villages but they carefully avoided Queenborough. The summary jurisdiction and the formidable cart-whip of the Mayor were worse than the court martial, the cat-o-nine tails and the Bosun's mate. The original cat-o-nine tails can still be seen in the Guildhall, Queenborough.

In 1832, on June 7th, under the Great Reform Bill, Queenborough was disenfranchised and could no longer send two members of Parliament to London, which it had done since the days of Queen Elizabeth I. One of the last two candidates for the Borough was Sir Thomas Gladstone, brother of William Gladstone, Prime Minister.

When King Edward III granted priviliges to Queenborough he thought it would become a great commercial port; but he was mistaken. As soon as they had acquired these boons, the Mayor and Burgesses sat down to enjoy them, and then commenced squabbling as to whom should individually reap the greatest benefit from them.

At the same time they carefully excluded 'foreigners', as they denominated persons born outside Queenborough, from the share. Although the liberty of sending two members of Parliament was obtained, the town did not improve and the petty squabbling continued until about 1840, when the last oyster was dredged up from the Swale and the Borough was £1,700 in debt, with a poor rate of 9/- in the pound.

In some old court books we find no crime so frequently punished as that of being 'a common butcher' or a 'common baker'; scolds too, and foreigners met with no mercy. One, John Clarke, was apprehended for being a Scotchman, as is supposed; and on this mere suspicion, it is commanded that he be kept in safe custody, but the mass of these records are an endless course of litigation concerning the rights of pasturing.

The Guildhall at Queenborough remains very much the same as it has been for centuries. It contains a magnificent collecting of Corporation regalia and other treasures.

High Street, Queenborough.

The massive mace is dated 1678, and is considered to be one of the finest in England. There is a smaller mace dated 1608, the Mayor's wand of office is unique, for it is believed to be a wand of olive wood brought home from the Holy Land by Sir John de Foxley, the first Governer of Queenborough Castle. It is enclosed in a silver case which was presented by Thomas Young Greet, Mayor, in 1818. Among this collection is the staff of office of the Water Baliffs in the form of a silver oar which disappeared mysteriously many years ago and turned up eventually at Sothebys a few years ago and was purchased by the Queenborough Council.

In the year 1885, during the reign of Queen Victoria, the town had a new charter of Municipal Incorporation, and the election of four Aldermen and twelve Councilors, from whom a Mayor is chosen annually was fixed for November. The original charter granted by King Charles I, expired in that year.

It is interesting to note the following figures:-
>In 1881, the population numbered 982.
>In 1889, the population numbered over 1,000.
>The number of houses in 1885 was 191, and in 1888,
>there were 215 houses.

In 1908, the carved alterpiece in Queenborough church was constructed from an oaken beam which is known to have come from Queenborough Castlle, the stones used in the restoration of the tower came also from the castle and were the gift of Mrs Pierson of Fig Tree House.

Queenborough in the 19th century had become an important port for passengers and freight bound for the continent and twice a day steamers were dispatched to Flushing, Belgium, Holland and Germany, this thriving port continued until 1912, when the buisiness was transferred to Folkestone.

During the two world wars which followed, Queenborough once again became a busy town, for minesweepers and other naval craft engaged in warfare were stationed there.

Today, Queenborough is a thriving industrial town. Potteries and chemical works are the chief industries. The American firm Abbott Laboratories, has established a modern factory there and a number of small industrial firms have increased the prosperity of the town.

The hopes of Queenborough becoming a great port are now being realised, for the old dockyard has become a prosperous commercial port and the future prospect is good.

No-one with imagination can walk down the High Street of Queenborough without remembering scenes of the past. For along this street passed pageant of English history, a procession of Kings and Queens, Noblemen, Men-at-Arms, Admirals, Captains and prisoners of war

There came Edward III and Queen Philippa with their retinue, hobe-liers, bow-men and knights in armour bound for Crecy and Agincourt, and there were fishermen from Queenborough, Leysdown and Minster, to sail against the Armada.

Queen Elizabeth I came to meet the nobility of Kent in the castle, Nelson and Lady Hamilton, Troubridge, Howe and the great admirals of the Napoleonic wars would have walked here. Indeed the people of Queenborough have a right to be proud of their ancient heritage, and whatever the future holds for them, we may be certain that the illustrious past of their Borough will be treasured forever and handed down to those that come after them, as a priceless heritage.

LIST OF THE CONSTABLES OF QUEENBOROUGH CASTLE

1336-1350	Edward III	John de Foxley - John of Gaunt
1378	Richard II	Robert de Vere, Marquis of Dublin Earl of Oxford. Sir Arnold Savage, Knight. William Scroope, Son of Lord Scroope.
1401	Henry IV	William de Waterton. John Cornwall, Baron of Fanhope Thomas Arundel, Archbishop of Canterbury.
1413	Henry V	Gilbert de Umfreville, Humphrey Stafford, Duke of Buckingham.
1483	Richard III	Thomas Wentworth. Christopher Colyns.
1485	Henry VII	William Cheyney, Sir Anthony Browne, Knight of the Garter.
1509	Henry VIII	Francis Cheyney, Sir Thomas Cheyney Knight of the Garter. Etc.
1558	Elizabeth I	Sir Richard Constable, Knight. Sir Edward Hoby, Knight.
1603	James I	Phillip, Earl of Pembroke and Montgomery

5 THE HISTORY OF SHEERNESS

In Domesday Rolls = to cleave or cut.. a headland cutting into the sea

In early days Sheerness was a mud flat, invaders avoided this place because the mud was too treacherous.

There is a possibility that a blockhouse built by King Henry VIII stood here, for in 1547, there existed at Sheerness a block-house or bulwark, as a battery was then called.

Queen Elizabeth ordered Sir John Gilbert to reorganise this battery in 1551. It was at this period that the beacon system of Kent was reorganised under the general order governing the whole country.

There were two beacons on Sheppey, one near the church at Leysdown and the other on the high hill between Eastchurch and the Swale. With the demolition of Queenborough Castle by Oliver Cromwell, the island was left defenceless. A need for a fortress to guard the Estuary was felt and a small fort of 12 guns was constructed by Sir Martin Beckman and Sir Bernard de Gomme.

Money had been freely voted for the purpose of strengthening the defences of the Medway, but it had been wasted by the King, Charles I. On June 7th 1667, when the invasion of the formidable Dutch fleet occurred, a great battle took place off Sheerness but the defenders were overwhelmed and Sheppey lay at the mercy of the enemy who sent three of their largest ships to attack Sheerness. The fort offered little resistance to the Dutch.

Nine of the twelve guns were unserviceable and the defence utterly broke down.

The Dutch took possession of the hulks and stores at Sheerness and removed goods to the value of £40,000. They received the submission of the Mayor and Corporation of Queenborough, who surrendered the town to save bloodshed. The small fort was entirely demolished.

On July 23rd 1668, when King Charles II, accompanied by Prince Rupert visited the Island where Sir Chichester Wray, who had been appointed Governor of the Fort on June 26th 1666, met them.

It was decided to rebuild the fort at once and it was completed in 1669.

Some of the cost was borne by the Corporation of London, who contributed the sum of £10,000. The fort was now renamed Garrison Point.

In 1673, an old privateer, Captain Richard Beach, as an appreciation for his services, was knighted and made Commissioner of Chatham and Sheerness. This old sea captain protested strongly against the conditions of the men at the garrison and the workmen at the dockyard, and did much to improve their lot.

On November 20th 1683, His Majesty King Charles II purchased of Edward Vernon Esq. twenty three acres of fresh marshland and seventeen acres of salt marshland and beachland.

There were at that time no houses or buildings on these forty acres.

From the year 1683, the Government Establishments at Sheerness grew in extent and importance and the town grew up side by side with them.

After the building of the Garrison Point fort, the attention of the Admiralty was turned towards the building of a naval dockyard at the mouth of the Medway. Sir William Winter, surveyor to the Navy, decided on Sheerness.

A small dockyard had been in existence here since 1665, when it was fitted up for the careening of naval ships, the work being carried out by workmen from Chatham 'yard.

Samuel Pepys records in his diary for 1665: "To Sheerness where we walked up and down, laying out the ground to be taken on for a 'yard, to lay provision for cleaning and repairing ships, and a most proper place it is for the purpose.....for it is a much better place than Chatham."

The Dockyard for a time consisted only of wooden and mud docks, but in 1708 a dry dock was completed. So far as Sheerness was concerned there was no town at all. A few houses had been built near the dockyard and at Blue Town, mostly made of wood.

There were Government residences in th garrison for the Governor, Lieutenant Governor and a few other officers and just enough men to man the fort, so the Government decided to utilise the old hulks which were used as breakwaters to protect the dockyard as lodgings for the workmen and their families.

After he had visited Sheerness, John Wesley wrote this account in his journal in 1767: "Such a town as many of these live is scarce to be found again in England. In the dock adjoining to the fort there are six old

'Men of War', these are divided into small tenements, forty, fifty, or sixty in a ship, with little chimneys and windows; and each of these contain a family.

"In one of them where we called, a man and his wife and six little children lived. And yet all the ship was sweet and tolerably clean; sweeter than most sailing ships I have been in.

"To this acquatic village were many convenient entrances from the land side and handsome bridges from the main deck of one ship to another. They had their King Street, Queen Street, George Street and Prince's Street, and many others.

"It was truly pleasant to penetrate the dwellings of those good wives who were cleanly. Out of the port-holes were their hanging gardens. If not so prolific as the hanging gardens of Alcinous, they were fully as useful to the laborious inmates, whose gratifaction arose from the humble salad and the simple flower.

"Within the apartment, the bedstead was turned up in a corner of the room, and neatly covered with a quilt as white as the driven snow.

"In another corner was fixed a buffet well stored with china cups and saucers, and a little silver plate, such as tea-spoons, and perhaps one for the table, the floor was spread with a carpet of matted rope: the fireplace was well secured from danger, and in all respects convenient.

"In every street was a midwife, with her name and profession fixed in the most conspicuous part.

"Hundreds of children had been born on board these breakers, and seven-tenths of the workmen of His Majesty's dockyard are not ashamed to own their aquatic birthplace.

"Thus would the wisdom and humanity of the State provide for its servants, and blend comfort with security."

In the year 1765, Sir Thomas Slade drew up plans for the development of Sheerness, and the "Alleys" were built, they were large barracks at first three and then four stories high, they were known as "Little Alley" and "Big Alley" and were occupied by dockyard workers and their families. At first the workers lived rent and rate free, but afterwards rent was charged and they were required to contribute to the dockyard workhouse, of which the "Foreman Afloat" was master.

More houses were built to house the officials, and a public house named the Three Tuns stood where the Admiral's garden was in later years. There was a tap house and a fish stall. The road out of the 'yard crossed the site nearly in a line with West Street. Sheerness had a market place and shambles then; the market was held every Saturday and frequented by country people, who did a good trade.

The market place was on a part of the Lower Camber, there were a few shops also. They stood on wheels inside the garrison, notably three kept by Cocking, the tailor, Connor, the shoemaker and Craig, the barber. This trio of tradesmen, Cocking, Connor and Craig were known by the wits of the period as "soap, leather and rag"; in pointed, if not complimentary, references to their trades.

In the year 1725, a young man named William Shrubsole came to work in the dockyard. He was a serious, religious man and was appalled at the lack of a place of worship, so he obtained permission to use the sail-loft in the dockyard each Sunday, and read the Gospels to those of his fellows who attended.

William Shrubsole established the first church in Sheerness by founding the Congregational Church in 1752. The Church first met in No 26 High Street, Blue Town, and was known as the "Old Meeting House".

It was here that John Wesley preached on December 5th 1769 and again on October 12th 1776.

The Church subsequently removed to a new church in Chapel Street, and afterwards to a converted hall in Hope Street, Sheerness.

The development of Sheerness was severly handicapped by the lack of drinking water, and most of that was brought from Chatham in tanks and barrels. In 1782, Sir T.H. Page, an officer in charge of the Corps of Engineers, was sent to Sheerness to sink a well. The drilling was most succesful, for after digging and drilling to a depth of 328 feet, the water rushed up to within 60 feet of the top of the well. It was of excellent quality and plentiful.

In this year, an act of Parliament was passed for fortifying the "Point". England was recovering from the troublous times that had been experienced and with ten years of peace, prosperity was etablished and Sheerness was growing fast.

The Commissioners of the Admiralty caused great discontent among the workmen of all the Royal Dockyards by taking away the privilege of "Chips", a pre-requisite greatly valued (and abused) by them.

Thieving was a general practice. The workmen appeared to have been robbing the Admiralty to make up their alleged arrears of pay.

The name Blue Town is attributed to the fact that the men were entitled to these "chips" as part of their pay. Tradition has it that these chips were often "prefabricated" and made the erection of a house quite easy, and the blue paint with which the houses were painted was purloined from the Admiralty stores. The name has stuck for Blue Town it remains to this day.

The dockyard was in those days a very busy place and one of the stories told of that time was this:- The sailmakers and blacksmiths worked Sunday and work-a-day from 5am till 10pm. One day, master John Bush, a blacksmith, asked the Master Shipwright for a days leave. "What for", enquired the officer. "Well sir", replied master John, "you see, I've got four children. I have seen 'em often enough by candlelight but never by any other way. I just want to see what they look like by daylight, that's all."

From a letter written in December 1792, we have a list of the workmen then employed in Sheerness 'yard:-

Sheerness. 22nd December 1792
Navy Board

Hon'ble Sirs - undermentioned is an account of the number of Artificers, workmen and labourers of all sorts now borne in His Majesty's 'yard here; pursuant to your directions of the 19th inst;
Viz:-

Shipwrights	71	Riggers	12
Caulkers	14	Sawyers	7
Blacksmiths	7	Blockmakers	1
Joyners	5	Quarter-boy	1
House Carpenters	23	Pitch-heater	1
Bricklayers	5	Ocham boys	5
Sailmakers	11	Bricklayers labourers	4
Scavelmen	17	Labourers	17
Teams	2	Braziers occassionly	2

Total 204. I am Sir........

The French Revolution in 1793 scared the people of England and once more she was prepared to hold her own, and in that same year England declared war on France.

More men were sent to Sheerness dockyard, and some help was contributed in fitting out the Fleet which, under Lord Howe, defeated the French at Brest, on June 1st 1794.

At this time Mile Town did not exist. A few scattered farm houses were the only buildings. No high road was formed through what is now the High Street. The high road to Minster ran along by the shore, outside of the present sea wall, in fact along the beach as far as Scrapsgate and thence around the foot of the hill.

Queenborough was reached by a bridle path, and so was King's Ferry, but no proper highway was formed into Sheerness from Kent until some years after this period.

A gentleman who visited Sheerness on business during the "Mutiny of the Nore" wrote that he had walked over and returned in a post-chaise, which had brought over some high naval officers to Sheerness respecting the mutiny. This post-chaise carried a boy on purpose to jump down and open the field gates which crossed the road at the boundary of each field, between Sheerness and the Ferry.

A story is told that in 1794, when we were at war with France:-

Suddenly one morning it was noticed that there were sounds in the air of a nature well known to the ears of many who then dwelt in "Old Sheerness". There was no mistake about it, there was a heavy engagement going on, not very far off to sea-ward.

The small military force was on the alert at once. The great guns were carefully looked to, shot and powder served out, and fires laid in the furnances to heat the shot withal. Still the booming continued.

Nothing could be seen, loud and close as the engagement evidently was. All day they waited on, anxiously expecting news of the great engagement that had lasted so many hours. The news never came, but the mystery was fathomed, nevertheless.

On the shore, ready for embarkation, lay a number of empty water tanks. A strong breeze was blowing and it happened to blow athwart the mouths of these iron tanks. Hence the sonorous booming, like great guns at a distance, and if the then Governor of Sheerness did not ask the man home to supper who found it out, and sent everyone off home to bed after an anxious day why, the Governor of Sheerness was wanting in his duty - that's all.

The account given of the Nore Mutiny of 1797 afforded glimpses of "Old Sheerness", which were very interesting to those who could realize them.

The great French Revolution was a new thing; every good church-going Englishman then, set down everything bad that happened to the occult influences from France. Great discussions took place at "The Fountain" or the "Granby's Head", on the victories that the English Admirals had won over the Spanish and Dutch navies, and the name of Horatio Nelson was beginning to be heard more often than any other.

This name was not unknown in Sheerness, for he served on the guard ship "Triumph" stationed at Sheerness. He learnt navigation while sailing small ships on the estuaries of the Thames and Medway. He later joined the frigate "Lowestoft" as second lieutenant. In 1785 he was appointed lieutenant on the "Boreas", also at Sheerness, and later given command of the "Agamemnon" in the Medway.

He had a house in Queenborough and took Holy Communion in the church there. His connection with Sheerness and the Medway continued all his life, and after his death, the "Victory" carrying his body, anchored off Sheerness, where his remains were transferred to the coffin made of the main mast of the "L'Orient" (captured at the Battle of the Nile) and finnaly to Greenwich, where the body laid in state.

But things were happening in Sheerness itself, for in May 1797, mutiny broke out among the men of the ships under Nore Command. The ringleaders came to the Commander in Chief, Vice Admiral Buckner and presented their demands, he refused point blank to look at them.

The men, angered by the refusal, manned their boats and made their way into the harbour, where they seized the gun boats lying there and sailed them out.

The brass band accompanied the mutineers to sea, but its repertoire was limited to "God Save the King", "Rule Britannia" and "Britons Strike Home" - hardly the proper musical accompaniment of a naval mutiny.

The red flag of mutiny was hoisted on board the "Sandwich", and every ship lying near Sheerness was obliged to join the mutineers at the Nore.

Every day the mutineers landed in great force at Sheerness, in proper procession, headed by the band.

The leaders were rowed round the fleet, and as they passed, every ship's company greeted them with loud cheers.

The mutiny took on the appearance of a gala, and Sheerness, or part of it, was "en Fete". Meetings were held in public houses, and ashore, the Chequers Inn became their headquarters. After every meeting there were celebrations and they were continued far into the night on board H.M.S. Sandwich.

The spirit of carnival was abroad, albeit the mask of tragedy was soon to follow. The seamen would march in procession straight through the dockyard without meeting any opposition at all. They even went into the garrison to enlist the sympathy of the soldiers there, interrupting the parades, accosting old friends on parade and generally making a disturbance while the officers dared not interfere.

A deputation from the Admiralty came down to meet the mutineers, hear their grievances, and deal with them.

The mutineers rejected the conditions laid down, and negotiations fell through. The people of Sheerness hitherto had been sympathetic towards the men, now they began to reconsider their opinion.

The Government were willing to negotiate, the men were not, so the rebels lost the sympathy and support of the people ashore.

When the delegates marched away with the red flag of rebellion still flying, feeling swung in favour of the Government. This change was so marked that the rebels no longer dared to land, and cut off from their supplies and communications the mutineers were soon in a sorry state.

The town prepared itself for an attack from seaward, and in order to prevent the mutineers from escaping out of the estuary, the naval officers destroyed buoys and navigation lights, so that they dared not risk taking the ship downstream.

The dockyard men were soon strongly opposed to the mutiny, and when the mutineers stormed on board the gunboat "Vesuve" and hoisted the red flag, the dockyard men went on board and replaced it with their own dockyard flag.

The end was in sight. Resistance was worn down through lack of supplies and the growing helplessness of their plight. On June 13th, sixteen ships surrendered, one after another, at Sheerness.

The next day the "Sandwich" came into the harbour and Vice Admiral Buckner arrested Parker, the ringleader. Four hundred other mutineers were taken into custody.

Parker was tried for treason and condemned to death. Each ship sent a lieutenant and a party of marines drawn up on the quarterdeck, to be witnesses of the execution.

Prayers were said and three psalms sung. Parker asked Captain Moss for a glass of wine; taking it he said: "I drink first to the salvation of my soul, and to the forgiveness of all my enemies."

He asked if the Captain would shake hands with him, which the Captain did. He now asked if he could say a few words. Consent being given, he said: "I wish only to declare that I acknowledge the justice of the sentence under which I suffer, and I hope my death may be deemed a sufficient atonement and save the lives of others." He then knelt down for a moment and, rising, he announced, "I am ready". Parker asked that the handkerchief be removed from his eyes, the Provost Marshall placed the halter over his head, and he was swung out on the yard-arm of H.M.S. Sandwich.

This happened at 9.30am. The body was lowered after hanging for half an hour.

Parker's body was immediately placed fully clothed in a shell and taken in one of the boats to the east point of the garrison, then carried to the new naval burying ground. Here the coffin lid was taken off, and the body was displayed to the spectators for a few minutes, and was interred exactly at noon.

The mutiny at the Nore sprang from a very deep sense of grievance, for the treatment of sailors in those days was extremely harsh, most of the sailors were press ganged or otherwise forced to serve afloat.

The ultimate consequences for the Navy and the dockyard, were good, as many injustices and hardships were brought to light and remedied, and legitimate grievances dealt with.

Before we leave this memorable year of 1797, the following list of officials resident in Sheerness during the mutiny may be interesting. It is extracted from a copy of "Debretts Kalender" for that year.

Among other information in the old book, we learn that the Members of Parliament for Kent were:Sir E Knatchbull, Bart: and Sir W Geary, Bart. Members for Rochester, Sir R King, Bart: and theHon. H Tufton.

The Members for Queenborough were, John Sarjent Esq. and Evan Nepean, Esq. The first Lord of the Admiralty was Earl Spencer, and Earl Howe was Admiral of the Fleet. The Hon. William Pitt was Prime Minister.

Sheerness Dockyard 1797

Under the inspection of F.J. Hartwell, Esq. during the War - £800

Clerk to Ditto - G. Everest - £80 Boatswain - T. Simmonds - £70
Clerk to Ditto - T. Ongley - £70 Surgeon - W. Murray - £100.
"besides his twopences".

Clerk of Cheque - H. Lawson - £150 - Mst. Boatbuilder - W. Hunt -£
Storekeeper - T. Grant - £150 Mastmaker - W Shrubsole
Mst. Shipwright - T. Mitchell - £150 Mst. Sailmaker - W Shrubsole
Clerk of Survey - E. Shrubsole - £150 Mst. Smith - S. Coveny
Mst. Attendant - James Fraser - £150 Mst. Carpenter - J. King
Mst. Shpwrts Asst - John Hooker - £80
Mst. Joiner - T. Morse
Mst. Caulker - John Hooker Mst. Bricklayer - W Halliday
Porter - J. Hill - £25

Ordnance Dept:

Storekeeper - William Akid - £100 Clerk of Survey - T.L. Pennel - £90
Clerk of Cheque - W. Chambers -£80 W. Breeze - £60
Clerk of Cheque - M. Dodd - £50
Governor of Garrison - Gen. Francis Craig - £300
Lieut. Governor - Sir James Malcolm - £182

Income tax was 2/- in the pound, the tradesmen of Sheerness were prosperous, as every week or two, frigates and warships put into the harbour, their crews with money to burn. An extract from an old document had this to say: "The "Impereuse", 36 gun frigate, came in yesterday to Sheerness harbour. At her masthead were tied three silver candlesticks. She has been dis-establishing and dis-endowing at the same time some church on her own account. Of course it was a foreign church which puts the thing in quite a different light. Five hundred pounds was paid down on the capstan yesterday, and the crew had fourteen days protection from the press-gang granted them.

Fourteen days leave was too long for £500 to last amongst "Jack Tars", as they were then. Very little of this £500 missed its way into the tills of the Sheerness publicans and tradesmen in the course of the next 48 hours. This is why a two shilling income tax was, after all, a bearable burden in

Sheerness in those times.

In the old days, before the dockyard wall was built, Blue Town was a very lively spot, especially when the sailors came ashore on leave. The number of public houses was out of all proportion to the civil population and they provided almost the only means of entertainment for sailors.

Most of the great sailors of that age would have been seen in Blue Town. Nelson, Troubridge, Cochrane, Collingwood, Hood, Howe and many others all came to Sheerness and patronised its inns and entertainments. They stayed at the Britannia Hotel, which is the oldest licensed premises in the town. It was rebuilt in 1891, but in those days it stood alone in the fields which surrounded the town, and was a coaching inn. The names of these illustrious sailors were entered in the visitors book, which was proudly treasured by the owner.

A number of celebrated men were born in Sheerness: W.H. Shrubsole, the geologist, had a business in Blue Town; Sir Nathaniel Barnaby K.C.B. was born there in 1829, he founded the Royal Corps of Naval Constructors, and was also a prolific hymn writer

Henry Russell, the musician, was born in Blue Town in 1812, he travelled widely and studied under Rossini. His two sons, Henry, the elder, was a great singer and operatic impressario. His second son took the name of Landon Ronald and became a great conductor and composer of international fame.

Apart from public houses, the only other entertainment in Sheerness was "The Theatre". This was a wooden building standing on a site now enclosed by the dockyard wall. Samuel Jerrold, with his family came to Sheerness to live. He rented this theatre for £50 per year.

The officers and men of the Royal Navy patronised it and all kinds of entertainments were provided for them. Among its patrons were Lord Cochrane, the famous Admiral, the Port Admiral and the Governor of the Fort.

One of the actors who appeared was Edmund Kean, the greatest Shakespearian actor of his day, who afterwards took London and Bath by storm. He joined the Sheerness Company in 1804, and his salary was 15/- per week. Kean told a friend that he was so poor at that time, that he tied his wardrobe in his handkerchief and swam over the Swale to avoid paying the ferry dues. He appeared again at Sheerness Theatre in 1807; this time his salary was a guinea per week.

Douglas Jerrold, the son of Samuel Jerrold, joined the Navy, but he left to take up writing for the theatre. He found a friend in Kean, who helped and advised him.

Jerrold wrote many successful plays and articles, and he became famous as the first editor of "Punch".

Eventually the old theatre was sold and the Jerrold family left Sheerness in 1815.

The mother of D.H. Lawrence, the writer, lived in Sheerness. Her father was an engineer in the dockyard and they lived in Neptune Terrace on the sea front.

In 1813 the work of rebuilding the dockyard was undertaken. The engineering work was entrusted to John Rennie, the great civil engineer. He supervised the construction until he died in 1821.

The old hulks were removed, and the problem of the soft mud was overcome by sinking obsolete vessels, and by the extensive use of piles to form a sound foundation. It was considered a great feat of engineering. Three docks were provided and the wall surrounding the 'yard was built at that time by the use of convict labour. The convicts were housed in the old ships anchored off Stangate Creek and Deadman's Island.

The work supervised by John Rennie, the younger, was completed on September 5th 1823 and opened by the Duke of Clarence, afterwards King William IV (the sailor King).

The day of the opening was a great one for Sheerness, when H.M.S. Howe was docked with great ceremony. It was witnessed by thousands of people who came from London and the country. There were many steam-boats and the town was gay with bunting. To crown it all many balloons came sailing over. They were then a great novelty.

It was about this time that the leading citizens of Sheerness petitioned the Home Secretary, Sir Robert Peel, to change the name of Sheerness to Clarence Town, after the 'Sailor Prince' who was so popular.It was turned down, however, because it was thought that to change the name would destroy the old associations connected with Sheerness. Admiralty House in the dockyard was built as a residence for the Duke of Clarence.

Sir Edward Banks had plans prepared to build an elegant town in Sheerness. He aquired much land and bought up old properties with that view in mind.

He designed the Broadway in 1827, (then known as Edward Street) and built himself a fine mansion, the grounds covering three acres of park land with many fine oak trees in them. This later became the Royal Hotel, and the cinema and the Victoria Working Men's Club were built in the original grounds.

He also built Banks Terrace, and had great plans for building a pier on the sea front near the Royal Hotel, he visualised Sheerness as becoming a sea-side resort of some note, but his plans were thwarted by the 'Oyster Fisheries Commission' and several leading citizens. For about twenty years Sheerness stood still, except for the building of a new pier in Blue Town.

The Crimean war brought Sheerness as a Naval depot into the fore, more residents flocked into the place, and more houses were needed.

The land belonging to Sir Edward Banks came on the market, and instead of dignified houses being built, workmen's dwellings were erected. Neptune Terrace was a slight improvement, and soon terraces of houses sprung up.

The United Land Company took over, and the chance of Sheerness becoming a prosperous watering place was gone for ever. Rows and rows of small dwellings were built, connected by numerous alley-ways, a hotch potch of uninteresting barrack like streets was created, and the dream of Sir Edward Banks was shattered.

A plantation of trees was planted on either side of Bridge Road, (now Halfway Road) in an attempt to beautify the approach to Sheerness, but they did not survive, and it still remains bleak and bare and uninteresting.

A famous ship, the 'Great Eastern', built by Brunnel in 1856, was based at Sheerness dockyard, she had six masts and five funnels and was the leviathan of her day. It was from Sheerness that she started to lay the first cable across the Atlantic in 1866.

In the year 1827, a fire broke out in Blue Town destroying fifty or sixty houses. On January 8th 1830, another fire took place and another fifty dwellings were burnt down, being made of wood nothing could stop the conflagration from spreading.

Trinity Church, the parish church of Sheerness was built in 1836. The first Garrison Church in the dockyard was built in 1667 and was burned down. A similar fate befell its successor. In 1881 the third church was also burned down, the fourth and the last church to be built was in 1885.

Saint Paul's Church in Blue Town was built in 1873, to accommodate the soldiers and their families when military units were quartered at Sheerness.

The Roman Catholic Church on the sea front was built in 1864, it came about in this way: A Colonel Moysten came to Sheerness with a corps of the North Cork Militia, whose principal characteristic was that it was composed of 'wild Irishmen' who were prepared to go through fire and water, once their blood was up. The Colonel, a Protestant, was proud to be at the head of his regiment on Sundays, and accordingly he march with them to Rose Street, where the Mass was celebrated, and where many of his men were compelled to kneel down in the road to witness its celebration.

So struck was the veteran soldier with the devotedness of his men to their native faith, that he had the Roman Catholic Church erected as it now stands, at the cost of several thousand pounds; the schools and the residence of the priest were also built by this Irish Colonel.

A memorial tablet to Henry Moysten and his wife is in the church. As well as the original Conregation Church there was also a Jewish Synagogue in Sheerness.

After the Nore Mutiny, the Admiralty began to look into the working conditions of the dockyard men more closely, and great improvements were made. In 1806 a workhouse was built inside the dockyard, and in 1843, a school was started for dockyard apprentices, Mr. Drew was the first schoolmaster.

The shortage of drinking water has been mention before, and in 1800, a well was sunk in the dockyard. Prior to this, water was conveyed from Chatham to Sheerness in a water tank called the 'Box Iron', which carried forty tons of water for the shipping and the Garrison.

Then the position was reversed. The water obtained from the Sheerness well was found to be superior to that of Chatham, and a water tank was built to take water from Sheerness to Chatham dockyard in 1807; the tank was named the 'Gantill' and it was used to supply the dockyard officers with water. In the early part of 1800, water from this well was taken to the Tower of London, so highly was it appreciated. It also supplied th 'yard', and the Garrison as well as the ships in the Medway.

When in 1860, the well that supplied the town dried up, water was purchased from the dockyard a 1d per bucket, so at noon and after work, some dozen or two water barrels, drawn by 'Jerusalem' or other ponies, might be seen in a long line nearly opposite the Duke of 'Clarence'.

Waiting their turn for a supply of the precious liquid, were assembled men and boys, impatient for their share , which came from a hose connected to the stand pipe coming from a kind of sentry box which stood by the wall.

Plans were put into operation to bring water in to the island, and it was decided to drill a well. Furze Hill Halfway was to be the site of the new water works.

In 1860, the railway connecting Sheppey to the rest of the world was finished. No longer need the inhabitants travel in 'Pratten's Van' to the Mainland, waiting on the 'hard' at the ferry until the ferry-man decided to take them across.

The ferry boat was a broad flat-bottomed vessel capable of taking on board four vehicles, and it was hauled across by rope laid from bank to bank, it was a slow progress.

No wonder, then there was tremendous rejoicing at the opening of the railway - prosperity would come to Sheppey, for they now had a bridge and a railway and everyone would be able to visit the world beyond the Swale.

Great was the excitement on July 18th 1860, when the first train came in, packed with celebrations, bands played, and twenty rounds were fired in honour; and pandemonium was caused when an empty cartridge landed in the last carriage among the top-hats and crinolines.

A grand dinner at the 'Royal Fountain Hotel' ended the great day.

But such was the mistrust of the islanders for 'new fangled' things, that for a year after the railway opened, Pratten's van still carried the mail daily to the Mainland.

Sheerness was growing. The population in 1861 numbered 16,000 and there were 1,600 houses, 32 public houses and 30 beer halls.

The dockyard was exceedingly busy. Up to a dozen ships at a time were being built or serviced there, and it would appear that the workmen in the 'yard were trained, and liable to bear arms if required, the men were very much under discipline, so that the dockyard was run more on the lines of a ship.

The dockyard came under the garrison administration and in 1848, there was at Sheerness a splendid Dockyard Battalion, under the command of Colonel Read, Master Shipwright. There was also a fine Boat Brigade, the services of which were at the Nation's call in time of need.

The dockyardmen of those days were long-livers, the average age of retirement being 68, while some served on until they were 75 years of age. With the increased activity in the dockyard, came a great demand for house accommodation and it became necessary to find development sites. One of the first, was a large garden opposite the 'Crown Hotel' in Mile Town, which in those days was a coaching inn. Close to it, standing back from the street, was an old farmhouse. This was transformed into Albion Place. Originally a toll-gate barred the roadway at this entrance to the town.

Edward Street was the limit of the town eastward, Trinity Church and the Royal Hotel were the extreme outposts. All beyond was marshland, except here and there a lodge or cottage.

The Sheppey Cottages stood on the sea front and furnished Hot and cold sea-water baths, for now people were becoming aware of Sheerness as a sea side resort. Cheyne Rock House, the residence of David Alston Esq: who owned the oyster beds, was quite out in the wilds.

This Mr Alston was one of the townsmen who objected to the building of the pier by Sir Edward Banks.

Beyond Cheyne House was a solitary cottage (now part of the Ship on Shore) where lived for many years a notable character - 'old Jesse Barton', shepherd and milkman, Barton's Point takes its name from this worthy of former times.

The intervening marsh was called the 'Hundred Acres', and the expansion of the town in this direction began with the erection of Neptune and Marine terraces, followed by Constantine Terrace, (now Alma Road), Alma Street, James Street, and 'the Fifties'. After that, Berridge Road and an extension of Alma Road to Cavour Road were made, but the greatest improvement was the construction of the esplanade.

There was much poverty and squalor in the town, many serious fights and disturbances took place, and the stabbing of sailors was a common occurance.

As one could imagine, it was lively, and many crimes were committed as general lawlessness prevailed. The authorities suggested that Sheerness deserved a resident magistrate. A Captain Fitzgerald was a magistrate in the dockyard, who dealt with offences, but crime was becoming so prevalent that his was insufficient.

During the 1860's there were two serious riots in Blue Town. On one occasion, forty soldiers advanced on the police station to rescue an imprisoned comrade. The police sergeant took a boat to Faversham to get help. In the meantime the mob broke open the jail, released the prisoner and wrecked the police station.

One Magistrate remarked that There did not seem to be another place in the whole of the world like Sheerness, a combination of Wapping and Whitstable, only a little worse than these dirty towns, a dirty, low, demoralized little Chatham.

There were many public houses; beer halls, and eating houses in the town, also numerous lodging houses. Among the more notable were - the Fountain hotel and Commercial Inn, the Wellington Inn, the Army and Navy Tavern, the Ship Tavern and Commercial Inn, the Parr's Head in Belle and Lion Street, the Bricklayers Arms, pleasantly situated at the bottom of Hope Street, open to the hills and the Medway.

The Mechanics Arms, and the Victoria were others, and the Crown Inn, which advertised port at 36/- per dozen bottles.

There were also thirteen bakers and thirteen butchers in the town. A bank was found necessary, and a house was used in Blue Town as the offices of the London and County Bank, later to become the Westminster Bank. It was a very common thing; for a trader of the town to entrust the payment of his wholesale London accounts to the Captain and owners of the barges sailing to and fro from London.

Education in Sheerness before the first Education Act of 1870, was provided by 'dame schools'. The dockyard had its own school for apprentices and a schoolroom was built on to the Bethel Chapel in Blue Town in 1838. There were a few private schools for the children of well to do parents, but nothing for the poorer children until the National School was built in the Broadway.

Entertainment, now, was provided by the Criterion Theatre, and many famous music hall stars began their careers in this theatre. The Mechanics Institute organised lectures, musical evenings and other forms of entertainment. 'Penny readings' were very popular. They were held weekly in the Co-op Hall and at the Literary Institute. This occupied the lower part of the premises at 84 High Street Mile Town until the Victoria Hall was built in 1868. The readings were then held in an upstairs room, the favourite author being Charles Dickens.

Magic lantern slides were shown at the Co-op Hall, and theatrical performances were given weekly by visiting companies. Musical concerts were in great demand, and once a year, 'Sanger's Circus' visited Sheerness with the extraordinary achievements of the Japanese, thrilling expoits of the serpent charmers, talented acrobats and graceful lady equestrians. So the play-bills advertised.

Outdoor sports were popular also, and the Royal Hotel running grounds were the scene of many a contest.

The local newspapers were the 'Sheerness Times' and the 'Sheerness Guardian', consisting of four pages of close print and costing 1d.

On April 4th, 1868, the Sheerness Times was enlarged to an eight page newspaper, and much correspondence of great length was published.

In 1869, the local papers were full of the rumours of the dockyard closing, and correspondence on this matter continued for months.

Nude bathing was a subject much discoursed upon. A lady wrote on the cost of crinolines, and lengthy articles were written on the subject, of shall woman have the vote; the question of the day is female suffrage.

Numerous letters were written in favour of 'Penny concerts' on Saturday evenings, many more were written about The wickedness of suggesting Sunday bands playing on the sea-front, and the nuisance and danger of hoop-playing on the public pavements was commented upon.

The population of Sheerness in March 1868 was 16,000.

The sentences passed on law-breakers in those days was appallingly savage. One man, George Clark, was sent to prison with hard labour for three weeks, for stealing an apple worth 1/2d.

On April 9th 1868, a woman named Frances Kidder was publicly hanged at Maidstone jail for the murder of her 13 year child, and another woman was sent to prison for gleaning a handful of wheat from a field. The owner stressed that she wasn't doing any harm, but he wanted to make an example of someone. The woman said she picked it because it was so pretty,

The sentence passed was seven days in prison, ultimately reduced to a fine of 5/6 and 8/- costs or jail for three days. The woman was unable to pay and subsequently went to prison.

With the coming of a new century, the prosperity of Sheerness increased and the opening of the Flushing - Queenborough Steam Packet Line brought many visitors to the town, for it was growing as a holiday resort.

Upon the death of Queen Victoria on January 22nd 1901, the whole country was in mourning, and on the 28th, King Edward VII was proclaimed King.

In 1902, the Sheerness tramway scheme was begun, and the land sales all over the island were in full swing. The new Light Railway from Queenborough to Leysdown was now in operation, and plots of land adjoining the railway were sold from £16 to £18 per plot, on a deposit of £1 down, the balance being paid by sixteen quarterly payments.

To celebrate the coronation of King Edward VII, it was proposed that a town clock be erected in the Broadway, and much correspondence for, and against, appeared in the local papers.

The Crescent, Sheerness-on-Sea.

On May 10th 1902, Dr W.G. Grace, the famous cricketer, hoped to bring a team from the London County Club to Sheerness, to play against the Wildfire Cricket Club on the Naval ground. The previous year he had played at Sheerness with the London Club and on that occasion the veteran champion scored a century. Unfortunately on May 10th, he was still playing at 'Lords', so his son, Mr C.B. Grace, deputised for him.

It is recorded that in 1902, the headmaster of Mile Town Boys' School, earned a salary of £145, rising by £5 annually to £170. this was a meagre pittance for such a responsible job and reflected the general poverty of the times.

The departure of the Bermuda floating dock built in the dockyard at Sheerness, was witnessed by hundreds of people in June 1902. About 600 tons of coal were stored in the dock as a reserve supply for the two tugs which were to tow her non-stop to Bermuda. The rate of progress was estimated at four knots per hour - and it is computed that if all goes well, the dock will reach Bermuda about the end of July.

Owing to the grave illness of the King, the coronation celebrations were cancelled, but the foundation of the clock tower was laid on June 26th 1902, the cost of which was estimated at £360, and the clock which was for many years over the Council Offices, would be utilised in the new tower, thus saving further expense. However, it was eventually discovered that the clock would not fit, so it was placed on the top of the Victoria Hall instead and a new one made for the Town Clock.

The census for 1911 showed an increase in the population of the town, for the numbers now registered 17,487 persons.

About this time there were rumours that the Flushing boats were to be transferred to Folkestone. This happened eventually in 1912.

The railway station at Blue Town was closed, and another built at Mile Town, which is still in use today.

During the 1914-18 war, Sheerness dockyard was a hive of industry and Blue Town was the first place in England to receive an aerial bombardment. This occurred on Christmas Day 1914 at mid-day, a solitary airman dropped several small bombs near the pier. No one was injured, but later raids caused the death of several residents in this part of Sheerness. Further raids occurred, Gothas and Zeppelins being used several lives were lost and property damaged.

Two terrible catastrophies occurred in Sheerness harbour during the

1914 war. It was on November 26th 1914, that the battleship 'Bulwark' was blown up, owing to an internal explosion, when over 600 lives were lost. On May 22nd 1915, the 'Princess Irene' was blown up from the same cause. She was a mine-layer and all the crew except one, numbering 1,078 officers and men were killed, along with 76 shipwrights, riveters and boys from the dockyard who were working on board at the time.

The 1921 census figures showed the population figures still rising they now numbered 18,673 persons.

Sheerness, considering its importance as a naval, military, and air base, was fortunate during the second World War. Eastchurch air-drome was bombed in the first phase of the Battle of Britain, and in the later stages of the war the flying bombs passed over Sheppey on their way to the London docks.

Concrete forts on stilts had been placed in groups in the estuary, an R.A.F. battalion was situated on the cliffs. Their combined gun-fire brought down a number of 'doodle bugs' before they could reach their objective. In the early stages of the war, Sheerness was evacuated of all civilians excepting those engaged in war work. The beach was covered with giant coils of barbed wire, concrete pill-boxes were built along the esplanade and a boom was placed across the mouth of the estuary. It was in a line with the Royal Oak Inn.

This boom was intended to stop submarines and mines from being laid. In spite of the boom, mines were laid and one of the pilot boats was blown up just off Cheyne Rock.

On June 18th 1944, a great armada of ships and parts of the Mulberry harbour could be seen from the esplanade, stretching stem to stern on the horizon, reaching from the boom to the mouth of the river.

Thousands of Sheerness residents watched this momentous gathering, and prayed that there would be no air raid that night.

In the morning, the craft were gone, save for one ship which had stuck fast on a sandbank, its three masts listing drunkenly against the clear sky. This was an American ship, the 'Richard Montgomery' and she was loaded with ammunition. Of course nobody knew it then, and speculation was rife, as at every low tide the M.T.Bs from Queenborough came in relays close to the ship and frantic unloading activities were seen to be going on.

For nearly a week this continued, as daily the 'Richard Montgomery' sank lower and lower into the sea and the operation was abandoned when at last at high tide nothing could be seen but the masts and the rigging.

It was not known until after the war that those gallant men on the little ships were unloading as fast as possible such a deadly cargo. This wreck is still visible off Sheerness, and there has been over the years great concern regarding it. Some amateur divers were exploring it. This reached the ears of the Admiralty and experts were sent down to look into the matter, and further explorations were forbidden. The Admiralty consider it too dangerous to blow up and think it better left undisturbed, but what the result would be if one of the huge oil tankers which operate from the Isle of Grain were to ram it by accident, it is impossible to say.

Returning for a brief moment to 18 June, from dawn onwards, the sky was filled with aircraft towing gliders. Hundreds and hundreds of them went over, and everyone was filled with awe and there was a tense atmosphere as people gathered on the wall to watch these unusual happenings, all speculating on their meaning.

Victory Day brought great rejoicing, and thousands of Sheerness people gathered round the clock dancing and singing until past midnight. The town was lit up for the first time since the beginning of the war. No one living in Sheerness at the time will ever forget May 8th 1945, 'Victory Day!

In February 1953, one of the worst floods ever recorded occurred in the town. From Half Way to Blue Town the streets were flooded to a depth of four feet. The marshes from the Swale to Scraps-gate were under water. Fortunately no lives were lost, but many sheep and cattle were drowned.

After this disaster, extensive work was done on the sea walls stretching from Leysdown to Queenborough, and a system of flood warnings was devised to deal with any future floods.

In 1951 another disaster occurred, the submarine 'Truculent' was leaving Sheerness dockyard after repairs when it was rammed by a cargo ship in the estuary. It sank, and there were no survivors. The submarine was eventually raised and put into service again.

In 1960, two very important events took place. The first one had widespread effects in Sheerness, for on March 31st 1960, the dockyard was officially closed. It was a sad and moving ceremony when the flag which had flown proudly over the dockyard for three hundred years, was hauled down for the last time.

The result of the dockyard closure was disastrous. The Island became a distressed area, for it had been the sole livelihood of the town. Unemployment was rife, shops, cinemas, and transport suffered; the High Street was deserted, no longer was the lunch hour and the evening rush hour a seething mass of people. There was an air of deep depression hanging over Sheerness.

It had been a sad day for many people. There was a hopeful note, however, for the second event promised a new lease of life.

On April 9th 1960, the new Ferry Bridge was opened by Princess Marina, the Duchess of Kent.

THE NEW AND OLD KINGSFERRY BRIDGES, ISLE OF SHEPPEY

The old bridge, built in 1860, had lasted a hundred years.

A toll had been levied on all users, as heavy dues were exacted by the Southern Railway Company as a return for the original outlay of constructing the bridge. In 1929, the Kent County Council purchased the rights from the Railway Company and the tolls were abolished. The bridge had been a source of inconvenience for a number of years. The cargo ships which had replaced the Thames barges carrying pulp to the paper mills were so large that they left only a few feet clearance on either side.

Consequently when they were blown off the course the lifting gear was damaged and the bridge remained out of action for sometimes weeks at a time. This disrupted trade and the life of the island considerably, as the access to and from the Island could only be obtained by boat, as in the old days, until the Bailey bridge was invented and then a spare one was kept on the marshes nearby as a precautionary measure.

At 9-50 on the great day, the last train passed over the old bridge and the new electric service was put into operation.

The new bridge was a massive structure, enabling the largest ship to pass through without fear of jamming the mechanism, and with a fine new road it was hoped that new industries would come to Sheerness.

Out of the first and largest, was the American chemical firm of Abbott Laboratories. The dockyard premises were taken over by the Harbour Development Company, and it is expanding into one of the finest commercial docks in the south of England.

This brought many new people into the Island and better class houses were needed and whole new estates have been built.

Several other factories have come to Sheerness which employ a number of woman. A steel mill has been built in the 'Well Marsh' grounds which employs hundreds of men.

In 1971. the garrison was disbanded, Admiralty House demolished and the last Dockyard Church is being used as a warehouse.

The old Police Station has gone, St. Paul's Church also, Trinity Road School, the first National school to be built in Sheerness is no longer standing. The Victoria Hall, later the Hippodrome, has been demolished and shops and offices built there.

The wooden houses in Blue Town have been replaced by blocks of flats. The imposing courthouse standing in fromt of the dockyard gates is up for sale. The old dockyard wall still remains but the South Gate, the guard house, and the Wildfire Naval buildings have all disappeared. Garrison Point is now a radar station operated by the Medway Ports, and serves the estuary well, for the building of a great oil refinery on the Isle of Grain has greatly increased the shipping in the estuary, and giant oil tankers use the lanes that once were the highways of the tall masted ships and the Royal Navy.

In some ways the closing of the dockyard was a good thing, for now the town can expand without the restricting influence of Naval and military occupation.

In 1970 the first Comprehensive School was built in Minster, housing 1300 pupils. The whole pattern of education has been altered and the experiment was being watched closely by the whole of the south of England. The school was officially opened by the young Duchess of Kent.

Another great change has taken place, for in 1967-8 the three separate councils which governed the island for so many years, have been amalgamated into one. It is now known as Swale Borough Council.

This amalgamation had been the source of controversy for a number of years. The Borough of Queenborough was at first bitterly opposed to the idea. However, progress must be made, and the old order changeth, time alone will tell if the change is for the better.

Sheerness in company with the rest of the island, has become a popular holiday resort, and there are several camps which provide seasonal work for the inhabitants.

The small family shops in the High Street have all become super-markets, and the Co-operative Society, the oldest, or second oldest, in England, has been taken over by the South London Co-operative.

All of the cinemas have been closed. The Rio has been knocked down and flats and houses have been built on the site, the other two are now a bingo hall and a Woody's night club.

The Meyrick Road Congregational Church which was unused for many years, is now Sheppey Little theatre and offers fine entertainment to all. The Boys Technical School in the Broadway, which has produced so many notable young men, has now been demolished and the pupils attend the Comprehensive School, a sports complex and an old persons home have been built on the site.

All the ancient buildings have disappeared, the small shops closed down and super markets built on the sites.

The face of Sheerness has changed completely and we can only hope that the new Sheerness which will eventually arise will be held in as great esteem as the old dockyard town.

6 THE HISTORY OF EASTCHURCH

Eastchurch in 1067 = Eastcyrce. 1431. Astchurche. Eastchurche

Eastchurch is written in the Domesday Monachorum of 1066-7 as Eastcyrce, it was subordinate to the paramount Manor of Middletune (Milton), subordinate to which is the Manor of Shurland which had anciently owners of that name. Shurland passed into the Cheyne family and from them to the Crown, thence to private ownership.

The Parish is so called because of its situation with regard to Minster, and consists of three Manors, Shurland, Northwood and Kingsborough.

It is situated on high ground, with the village nearly in the centre of the parish. About half a mile to the eastward of the village stands the remains of the Manor House of Shurland.

The Parsonage is about half a mile to the southward of the village.

Old records tell us that in the year 1190, Pope Celestine confirmed the gift of this former Church to Dunes Abbey. (The first Church was built by the Abbot of Dunes , (Dunquerque Belgium). In Lambeth Palace library there is an entry of the appointment of William de Wylton, who was instituted by Archbishop Peckham in August 1279.

In June 1300, the Vicarage was endowed with 11 1/2 acres of glebe, (long since appropriated by somebody else) and a rent of 8/- per annum. The Abbot and Convent of Dunes held the right of advowson until 1315, and then transferred it to the Abbot and Convent of Boxley, near Maidstone, as being the only Convent of the same order (Cistercian) as themselves in the County of Kent.

This transfer was duly carried out under the direction of Archbishop Reynolds. Thus the connection between Dunkirk and Eastchurch can be traced back six hundred years to the first Church built in Eastchurch.

The actual site of the original Church has never been located, but it may have been in the vicinity of Parsonage Farm. The present Church and parish came into being in the year 1432 when it was fully privileged as a distinct Parish Church.

The Northwoode family, at that period, held large possessions in Eastchurch. Sir Roger Northwood's Chaplain, Richard Sheme, who became Vicar in June 1353, was on one occasion required to testify that from the very early marriage of Sir Roger to Julians de Saye, their first child, Sir John de Northwoode was baptised in 1321, before Sir Roger had completed the fifteenth year of his age.

Some time before 1430, the second Church built at Eastchurch had decayed and was now a heap of ruins. William Cheyney, Lord of the Manor of Shurland, and the chief person in the parish, took steps in the matter; the large garrison of soldiers and their wives and children that were kept at Shurland, were seriously in want of spiritual provision, so he consulted with his great neighbours, the Northwoodes, Mr Robert Manne, and other friends, and they resolved to communicate at once with the Patrons, the Abbot and Convent of Boxley, to see what could be done.

Accordingly the Abbot and one or two of the Brethren came riding over the King's ferry to inquire into the question, and after deliberation it was agreed that the new Vicar should be William Nudds known by the Abbot as a man taking great interest in all buildings, and very methodical in all his ways - who should design a new Church and act as architect during its erection, instructions being given to him that he should work in the frames of the three windows of the old church that were in good preservation, and such other materials as he found fit.

But then arose another question. The old foundation was rotten.

The Church ought to be close to Shurland, and to the cluster of cottages lying between that house and its appendage, Little Shurland, or the 'Parsonage', as well as being nearer the great house of the Northwoodes.

That question William Cheyney soon answered by offering at once to give sufficient ground for a Church and Churchyard to the Abbot and the Brethren for this purpose, and to allow them that corner of his Shurland property that was on the east side of the village, and at the junction of the Leysdown and Warden roads.

The Abbot at once took steps to obtain the licence from the King, for permission to accept the land and build the church.

On November 16th in 1430, the licence was sealed, and by the end of the year the land was given over into the possession of the Patrons.

Soon William Nudds was at work. Masons could be supplied from the lay Brethren of the Convent,and he knew that if that supply of skilled labour should fail him, he could apply to some of the travelling guilds of stone cutters, to help him out.

One thing he had made up his mind about. The new Church whose Anniversary Day should be November 1st - All Saints Day - should be protected, so far as human care could manage it, from the fate of its predecessors, the weakness of the foundation should never be brought forward as a reason for any yielding in his work.

Accordingly the ground presently seemed scored with broad deep ditches, and many horses were seen coming up from the Windmill Quay laden with blocks of chalk, sent over by the eager Abbot of Boxley.

Into these ditches did William Nudds have the chalk thrown, and smiling to himself as he heard the people wonder what could be the meaning of this trouble.

The ditches filled, the ground began to be covered with stones; some of them undressed, also brought up from Windmill Quay, where they had been conveyed from the Maidstone Valley; others of them from the ruins of the old Church.

EASTCHURCH PARISH CHURCH, ISLE OF SHEPPEY   K 3044

And so, after a solemn service commending the building and workers to the care of god, the walls began to rise. At every corner, even of the porches, a buttress sprang. At the west-end of the tower an unusual work was determined upon, and that was to erect a porch against the tower, which should act as a huge buttress, and that in it should be inserted two Norman Slit windows which were among the ruins, and had formed part of a Church even older than the one which had fallen down.

And so the Church was finished, and was dedicated in 1432, and William Nudds was the Vicar until 1436.

It has a Nave and Chancel, each with two Aisles. There are two 'Ogee Arched squints' or hagioscopes, for affording a view of the High Altar from the two side Altars.

The panelled ceiling was painted, the tie-beams continue down the side walls with curved brackets which rest on Angel corbels in the Nave and Chancel, but stop square in the aisles.

There are central bosses with Angels having outspread wings. Near the south door of the Church stands an alms-box, on a tall stem, all carved out of solid oak. It has three locks, the keys of which are held, one by the Rector, and one by each of the Churchwardens.

In the year 1450, the County of Kent broke out in open revolt against the manner in which their political rights were being destroyed. Led by Jack Cade, and backed by an army of 20,000 Kentishmen, they attacked London and beheaded Lord Saye and Sele the Lord Lieutenant, and William Crowmer, the Sheriff of Kent, Lord Saye lived at Rushenden Manor, and William Crowmer at Borstal Hall.

Jack Cade requested a Charter of Pardon for his followers and most of them returned home, but Cade with some of the rebels attacked Queenborough Castle. He was unsuccessful, however, and fled to Sussex where he was killed.

The Charter of pardon revealed the names of Sheppey men who had followed Cade, one which stands out is:- Cheyne John, of Eastchurch in the Isle of Sheppey, the son of the William Cheyne of Shurland, who had given the building site of the new Church.

Others were as follows, - John Lymons of Minster, in the aforesaid island, husbandman, and all others from the Island:- John Cokeran, the Mayor of the new town of Queenborough, Yeoman; Will Baker, baker, and Will. Britte, John Britte, John Masyn; Will Canon; Alarus Jacob; Galfurs Benet; Robt. Sunster; John Willys; who are all described as mariners.

In the year 1559, the Lord of the Manor of Shurland, Sir Thomas Cheyne, died. His tomb is in the Abbey Church of Minster. He was a remarkable man, and held great offices during four reigns. A favourite of Henry VIII, he acquired great wealth and Manor after Manor was given to him, including the monastery, farms, windmill and appurtances thereof, of the dissolved Abbey at minster. He changed his religion to suit each reigning Monarch, and died during the reign of Elizabeth.

His only son Lord Henry Cheyne, inherited all his father's vast wealth and possessions, squandering it all in riotous living, selling Manor after manor, and exchanging his ancestral home, Shurland Hall, with the Queen for lands at Tuddington. He pulled down the Abbey and used the stones to build a new mansion at Tuddington, selling the gatehouse and land and the remains of the Abbey to Sir Humphrey Gilbert.

Thus Queen Elizabeth became Lady of the manor of Shurland, soon the cry of neglected tenantry and deserted farms reached her ears and viewing the now deserted Shurland and the depopulated parish of Eastchurch she resolved to look into the matter.

The Queen made an effort to bring back prosperity to Eastchurch by creating a remunative industry, she granted a licence for leather production. - to transport, subject to payment of custom, not more than 4,000 sheep felts, 2,000 sheep-skins, and 4,000 lamb skins.

The now defenceless state of Sheppey, deprived of the garrison at Shurland was dangerous, so to strengthen the Island she granted a lease in 1580, to a tenant farmer of Shurland Hall with this stipulation:- That the tenant shall convert. Ten of the outer chambers or rooms of the said house into tenements, and newe-build on the premises five other tenements, and in them to place ten able men to serve with caliver, pike, bowe, and such other like weapon for the defence of the Island; - and in the residue of the said house some honest and sufficient person with his family to dwell, and it shall be lawful for her Majesty, if she pleases, to take down and sell certayne of the outer houses there, being superfluous.

Thus this noble house became a barracks and a tenement dwelling, and the last quoted clause explains how in the course of time the old mansion fell into a state of ruin.

In 1511 Lord Henry Cheyne sold Parsonage Farm to Robert Livesey the grandfather of Michael Livesey. In 1584 Robert Livesey held the Rectorial rights and benefices of Eastchurch. his son Gabriel Livesey occupied the house and probably rebuilt it, the Arms of the Livesey's with that of gabriel's Wife, Anne Sondes were carved over the great mantlepiece, they were as follows:- Argent, a lion rampart gules between three trefoils vert, impaling those of his wife, Argent between two chevrons, three Moors heads Sable.

Sir Michael Livesey, the only surviving son of Gabriel, was born at Parsonage Farm and lived there all his life, he was created a baronet at the age of sixteen, and resented the King's taxes on his property. He is renowned as a regicide, for when at the age of 34 he sat upon the Commission of justice which condemned to death King Charles I, his name was prominent among the signatures.

During the Civil War, he commanded the Roundheads of the Kentish Horse, and was solely in charge of the Weald, he captured the village of Yalding and sacked Canterbury. He was member for Parliament for Queenborough with Augustine Garland, another regicide who signed the King's death warrant.

At the Restoration, Sir Michael Livesey fled to Holland to escape trial for high treason. He was captured and killed. His estates were forfeited to the Crown, and his old home Parsonage Farm, was given to James, Duke of York, later to become King James I. His wife Lady Elizabeth Livesey andher two daughters retired to Maidstone.

The ancient Parsonage was alienated by the Patrons of the benefice.

The Rectory and avowson was granted to Charles II, who united the benefice of Warden to that of Eastchurch.

The magnificent tomb of Gabriel Livesey and his wife, stands in the Chancel of the Church, the kneeling figure of the boy is that of Michael Livesey.

The oldest book of Churchwardens accounts dates back to 1663, and we note a few entries:- In 1665, 6/- was paid for making a ditch round the Churchyard. The Vicarage house then stood close to the road in the eastern corner of the Rectory garden, and in 1678, 5/- was paid for a bridge to lay at the style against Mr. Eaton's (the Curate) door.

In 1666, 6/6 was handed to the Archbishops Officer as the relief given by the parishioners of Eastchurch for the fire in London.

1667, 6d is paid for an hour glass, this was placed in the pulpit, to remind the Minister of the flight of time, and we occasionly read of a popular preacher whose congregations would call to him to turn it again, when they saw that the sand was nearly run out.

Some accident seems to have happened to this particular glass, because in 1670, the same sum was paid for a second. How long this lasted, or the custom was kept up we have no information but as no mention is made of a glass in the inventory of Parish goods taken in 1759, we may suppose that the custom had died out.

Entries are made of money paid to the dog whipper. He was an officer of some importance in olden days, and we find mention of his office in many parts of England. It seems to have been his duty either to keep dogs out, or to keep them in order if they came in to the church.

In 1670. 4/- was paid for mending of the stocks, we have no information about the number of times it was necessary to make use of them, but there seems to have been some wear connected with them, as in 1682. 8/- was paid for repairing them and the horse block, and in 1713. a new payer of stocks cost no less than £2- 6s-1d.

In the old days, instead of the garden between the Crooked Billet and the bakehouse, there was a triangular piece of waste ground; upon this the stocks were placed, and were thus in a very central position, and the unfortunate wrong doers placed therein the observed of all observers.

Every year on Ascension Thursday, the beating of the bounds of the Parish took place. The Beadle had a certain number of boys in his charge that day, who were soundly whipped at certain points on the boundary lines, so that they might have good reason for remembering in future the exact spot to which the parish extended.

These occasions called for refreshment, for the accounts show that in 1678. 6/- was paid for drink and in the year 1689. on April 11th, the Coronation Day of the two Monarchs King Will, and Queen Mary, was one of rejoicing for no less than the sum of £1-3s-0d was spent at Eastchurch for ye ringers for ye bere and ye bonfir.

The Eastchurch bells were rung on every occasion possible, and the ringers were always paid for refreshment.

The rejoicings for the coronation were kept up annually, and in 1693. £1-18s-0d was allowed for furze and beer.

In 1695, when William of Orange was on the throne, a tax was imposed on births, marriages, and deaths, a wag, calling himself Old Squib wrote these lines:-

Should foreigners staring at british taxation
Ask why we still think ourselves a free Nation,
We'll tell him we pay for the light of the sun,

For a horse with a saddle, to trot or to run,
For the flame of a candle to cheer the dark night
For the hole in the house if it let in the light;
For births, weddings and deaths; for our selling and buying,
Though some think 'tis hard to pay three pence for dying.

The tax was graded according to social status; thus a Duke paid £50 at a christening and an Earl £30, and whereas a bachelor Duke paid £12, a bachelor or widower of low estate only paid 1/-. the general tax on baptisms was 2/-, 2/6 at marriage and 4/6 at burial.

All through the 1700's, money was paid out for church repairs and equipment. In 1730, the panelled ceiling was painted, and the two brass chandeliers were made.

The bells were rehung, and the church roof patched up many times, until in 1801 a Church rate was levied for the special purpose of re-roofing it. The rate was 1/8 in the pound for the first year and 8d in the second.

A Mr Jaques was paid nearly £200 for re-leading the roof, and it says a lot for his workmanship for the same roof is still on the Church.

The south Chancel was used as a day school for many years.

In 1834, there was a disastrous cholera epidemic. So many people died that they were buried in a mass grave in the Church meadow, one of the victims was Sir Richard King, Commander of the Nore. His tomb is beneath the Altar in Eastchurch Church.

In 1835, the old Rectory was demolished and the new one built on the site of a forge and cobblers shop, adjoining the Church.

On May 13th 1840, Robert Stayner Holford Esq: of Shurland Hall gave a piece of ground, part of Shurland meadow, to the Church for all time, to build a school for teaching the children of the poor inhabitants to read and write and otherwise for instructing them ... etc. so the National School was built and still serves its purpose to this day.

In 1897, the Jubilee of Queen Victoria was celebrated at Eastchurch on June 24th. The proceedings began with a most hearty service at the Church which was crowded. The band of the 1st Kent Volunteer Artillery led a procession of children to Shurland meadow, where they dispersed to enjoy themselves in the swings, on donkeys, and in sports and games, each had a Jubilee mug.

The weather became stormy and the wagons from Leysdown and Harty began to collect their happy loads, everybody declared it was the most successful gathering they had known.

The village was very gay with flags, the school and meadow tastefully adorned by the decoration committee. The beef provided (about 100lbs) was boiled by the committee ladies, the ham (140lbs) was also cooked by them. About 700 adults sat down to tea and 300 children.

The water supply at Eastchurch had always been poor, but it appears that in 1905 it had improved,for the water butts which were placed around the church to catch the rainwater, had been removed as they were no longer necessary.

In 1901 great events were happening at Eastchurch, for on the 24th September, an Aero Club for ballooning was formed at Leysdown by Mr Brabazon, now Lord Brabazon. In 1906, the Short brothers joined the club and became official 'Balloon Engineers' for the Aero Club, they decided to manufacture aeroplanes, and built six machines for members.

Flying Ground, Eastchurch, Sheppey.

Mussel manor Clubhouse, Capel Fleet, the sea and the Swale were the borders of the original aerodrome at Shellness. On May 2nd 1909 the first flight of 100 yards was made by Lord Brabazon at Shellness.

The pioneers had great difficulties with the uneven ground and under-carriages, and a move was made to Eastchurch on November 20th 1909.

Stonepitt Farm and 700 acres of land was purchased by Mr Frank Maclean, a member of the Aero Club, and by April 1910 the move was completed.

Mr Dunn, conducting tests with his D.5. was the first pilot to write notes while flying; a high levelflight was first achieved in 1910.

On June 2nd 1910. C.S. Rolls made a double crossing to France - Dover 6-30, over france 7-15,returned to Dover at 8 o/clock. This was the greatest achievement in his career. He died in an air crash in July, by falling out of the machine at a height of 50 ft, he was the first man to be killed in an aircraft.

Mr. Sopwith came to Eastchurch in 1910 to win the De Forrest prize of £4,000, by flying 169 miles non-stop. He set up the Sopwith Aviation Company. This advent of the Aero Club promised prosperity for Eastchurch and houses were built to house the workmen, and many local men obtained jobs at the airfield.

Mr. G.S. Grace was the second aviator to lose his life at Eastchurch. In 1911, the Army became interested in the Aero Club, and in January 1911, two planes were offered to the Royal Navy to train pilots for aviation, 200 officers volunteered, but only four were required. The courses started on March 1st with two machines in use.

On August 16th 1911, the then World record for a duration flight was made, 4 1/2 hours in the air.

In 1911 also, Messrs; Short Bros produced twin-engines for aircraft. In September of that year the Naval Authorities established a flying training school for the Royal Navy.

The Hydro Aeroplane was invented on January 12th 1912, a take off from H.M.S. Africa was made. Longmore covered 172 miles, being four hours in the air, and won the Naval prize.

On May 13th 1912, the Royal Flying Corps was formed under the joint control of the Army and the Navy, but the naval Authorities wanted sole control.

In May 1912, a flight took off from H.M.S. Hibernia while the ship was making 10-15 knots.

The Air Dept was formed in 1912. In May 1913, Hermes became a Naval Establishment. on May 11th 1913, a Pinze-Nez aeroplane crashed at Queenborough.

In 1913, for the first time, aeroplanes were used in naval manoeuvres, it was a full dress rehearsal of the 1914 war. Wireless signals were used here for the first time. During the 1914 War, women were employed at the aerodrome and formed the original W.R.A.C.S.

The Aerodrome was subsequently taken over by the Royal Air Force. It was severely bombed during the second war in 1940.

At the end of the war the aerodrome was disbanded, and the premises were used as a transit camp for displaced Anglo-Indians after the Independence of india was accomplished.

It became an open prison in 1952, and continues as such today.

A very fine Memorial was placed in Eastchurch village, opposite the Church. It commemorates the pioneer aviators and depicts some of the early flying machines they used.

A beautiful and unusual stained glass window is in the Church, in memory of the Hon: C.S. Rolls and Mr. G.S. Grace. The first two pioneer airmen who lost their lives at Eastchurch; the fund for this window was started by Mr. Moore Brabazon and the Hon: M. Egerton.

Here is a report of the first great race at Eastchurch:-

July 1st 1911, The Gordon Bennett Race was a memorable day in the history of Eastchurch, some 7,000 people added to the population, happily the day was fine and no serious accident took place, Mr. Hammel, whose fall caused a thrill among the spectators, escaping with slight injury.

The motor cars, cycles, and pedestrians returning home in the evening, made our usually quiet village street remind us of a busy London thoroughfare. So far as it is known, we all behaved well, as a large detachment of police, with a Company of Royal Engineers kept us in order. The Committee has sent a donation to the St Johns Ambulance Brigade (Sheppey division) in appreciation of the excellent services rendered on the occasion. Donations have also been sent to the Eastchurch Boy Scouts, and two sections of the Sheerness Scouts, in recognition of their useful work.

The committee wish to record their thanks to the neighbouring farmers for the assistance rendered to the Club, and especially to Mr. A Boorman, of Hook Farm, who collected a charge from people coming through his farm, and handed it over to the Club on the same evening.

And so history was made. The small village of Eastchurch saw the birth of the aeroplane, and became the cradle of aviation in England.

Through the centuries, the farmers tilled the land, the soil being stiff

London clay, as was the rest of the Island, the crops being mainly wheat and beans, and the upland pastures being used for breeding and feeding the renowned Sheppey sheep, and through the years, sheep-shearing matches and ploughing contests were held annually until the coming of machinery replaced the horse for ploughing.

Now holiday camps have sprung up in and around Eastchurch, and in the Summertime, crowds of Holiday makers throng the quiet village street. In the winter it sinks back into silence once again to await the return of the migrating visitors.

7 THE HISTORY OF LEYSDOWN

Lesduna in Latin. Leswe Saxon. Leetdown. All mean the High Pasture.

The Parish contains the two Manors of Leysdown, the chief of which, is styled without any addition or distinction, the Manor of Leysdown. It seems to have been given by King Henry II (1154-89) to Holy Trinity, now Christ Church Canterbury, at the value of £25 yearly rent. Accordingly the Prior of Christ Church, in the 7th year of King Edward I (1278) claimed, and was allowed all the privileges of the Manor there.

Traces of this ownership still remain, for the rising ground between the church and the village, and the barn at its north base, are called Priory Hill and Priory Barn.

The monks of the Priory were responsible for the repair and maintenance of the sea wall.

King Edward II by his charter dated July 14th. 1317. granted to the Prior and Convent of Christ,Church and their successors for ever free waren, i.e. the right to preserve game in all the demesne land which they possessed in this parish, among others in the 30th year of his grandfather, Henry III.(1246), and the Manor continued in this situation until the dissolution of the Priory by Henry VIII.(1539) when it was with all the land and possessions of it surrendered to the King.

It was entered in the inventory as being worth £98-9s-2 1/2d.

The Manor did not remain long in the King's possession, as in the year 1541, he exchanged it for other land with the newly created Dean and Chapter of Canterbury, part of whose possessions it remained up to the beginning of this century.

Between the years 1541 and 1790, the Manor was held by the following lessees, Thomas Spylman and Martin Purefey, when in the reign of James I. it passed to one Thompson, and from him to Harris, who held it until 1741, when George II was on the throne.

The lease expired and was not renewd, so in 1742. the Dean and Chapter vested it in trustees for their joint uses; by then it was, in 1743. assigned to the Rev. Julius Deedes, and by his heirs to Sir John Filmer of East Sutton, Baronet, who married Dorothy, daughter of the Rev. Julius Deedes.

Between the years 1796 and 1837 we have no record of the lessees, but at the latter date it was held on a lease of 21 years by Thomas Ford Esq, owner of a large part of the parish of Leysdown, including Muscles, now called Mussel or Muswell, Nutts Farm and Lower Paradise Farm.

Nutts Farm was originally known as Notts Manor, from a family of that name who were the owners up to the time of Edward IV (1461-85).

It then passed to the family of Bartholomew, who owned it up to the time of Henry VIII, duringwhose reign it was transferred to Sir Thomas Cheyne. His son Lord Henry Cheyne sold it to Christopher Sampson in 1561, Anthony Sampson, his son sold it with Bartholomews Farm and Churchfield to Stephen Osborne, a benefactor to the parishes of Leysdown, Eastchurch and Warden; from his family it passed to Leonard Brandon, and then to the four daughters of Sir John Hinds Cotton; after which it was conveyed to Edward Jacobs. F.R.S. of Faversham. This was in the year 1752. Edward Jacobs was a learned naturlist and a skilled antiquarian, he wrote many books on the subject, among them being Fossilla Shepeianna, or fossil bodies of the Isle of Sheppey. Mr Jacobs also made many interesting discoveries - one of them, the spinal vertebrae, and a thigh bone of an elephant found in the clay at Minster cliffs, another, an elephant tusk, measuring eight feet long and twelve inches round, this was discovered at Nutts Manor itself.

At some later date, about 1839, it came into the possession of the afore mentioned Thomas Ford Esq, from whom it passed to Captain Hilton in 1888, thence to his heirs.

In the years after the 1914-18 war, it was used as a camping ground for holiday makers. Later the Council purchased the farm and in the 1960s the old manor house was pulled down and holiday chalets built on the land, it is now known as Nutts Camp.

Bartholomews Farm was sold by Osborne to Christopher Finch, and by him to Thomas Stephens,from whom it passed to his son-in-law James West and from him to John Sawbridge, another member of that family, Samuel Elias Sawbridge, was the owner in 1837.

The second Manor of Leysdown, known as New House, was anciently part of the possession of that branch of the family of Grey seated at Rotherfield, Oxfordshire, a descendant of which, John de Grey,was owner of it during the reign of Edward I, in the 25th year of whose reign (1297) he was summoned to Parliament among the Barons of this Realm. He died in 1312 and was succeeded by his son John, Steward of the King's Household.

During this King's reign he was also summond to Parliament.

His son, another John, was summoned to Parliament in the reign of Edward III. He was succeeded by his son Bartholomew de Grey. Upon his death, his brother Robert de Grey held the Manor until the year 1400 (Henry IV). When he died his daughter Joan, and her husband Sir J Deincurt inherited it. They had one son and two daughters of whom Alice, the wife of William Lovell, entitled her husband to this Manor. He was summond to Parliament from the 3rd to the 33rd year of the reign of Henry VI (1425-55).

His grandson Francis, Lord Lovell, was created Viscount Lovell in 1482 (Edward IV) and became a favourite of Richard III, on whose side he fought at Bosworth Field, (1485).

After the battle, he fled the country. Upon his return in support of Lambert Simnel, he was killed in the battle of Stoke-by-Newark in the reign of Henry VIII.

In 1485 an act of Parliament was passed for the conviction and deprivation of civil rights etc of Francis, Viscount Lovell, among others of King Richard's adherents, and the Manor was granted by the Crown to William Cheyne of Shurland, whose grandson Lord Henry Cheyne exchanged it for other property.

It can be seen therefore, that this small hamlet with its wealthy Lords of the Manor, has for hundreds of years played an important part in the history of England.

Leysdown Church

From a short extract in Hasted's History, written in 1782, we read thus, - There is no village or anything worthy of note except Nutts Manor.

Leysdown is a Vicarage with the perpetual Curacy of Harty.

It was given with its appurtenances by Robert de Arfi to the Priory of St. Radigund at Bradsole near Dover with the consent of Archbishop Stephen Langton, (1151-1228) and confirmed by Henry III. At the dissolution of the monasteries this Priory was worth only £98-9s-2 1/2d. Its possessions became vested in the Crown, and in the same year they were exchanged for other lands belonging to the Archbishop of

Canterbury, and have remained in the possession of the Archbishop since that date.

The historian, Hasted, describes the church - The Church of Leysdown is dedicated to St. Clement, and was in a most dilapidated condition until within the last few years.

The tower is of good workmanship and embattled, it hung over to the south more than seven feet out of perpendicular like that of Pisa. The body appears to have been much larger but had many years ago fallen down. Service was for some time performed in a shed built for that purpose. In a room of this, a small, neat, building of one aisle has been erected a wooden turret at the west end for one bell.

There is a space of two or three yards between it and the remaining part of the old tower, which has been taken down to within eight feet of the ground. What remains suffices to show its antiquity and costliness. Thus Hasted recorded in the year 1782.

A memoranda on the first page of the earliest register reads thus:- The Parish Church of Leysdown in the Isle of Sheppey and County of Kent, was rebuilt in the year of Our Lord 1734, at the expense of the parishioners and by benefactions to the amount of sixty pounds and upwards, procured from the Most Reverend His Grace William Wake, Lord Archbishop of Canterbury, the Revd, the Dean and Chapter of Canterbury and others. by John Woodroofe. Vicar. This £60 and upwards church, was built to replace the ancient church which was in ruins.

That the original church was ancient cannot be doubted, for in the year 1355 the Vicar, William de Riphil, was in trouble with the Abbess over burial fees. In spite of her orders that all burials must take place at Minster, he set the Abbess at defiance and buried certain bodies in the churchyard at Leysdown.

Some busy-body carried the news to Minster, and great was her indignation. The Vicar, who had his people behind him, told the Abbess politely but plainly what he thought about her action in the matter. The Abbess appealed to His Grace Archbishop Islep's legal auditor, who admonished the Vicar and imposed a fine.

At the dissolution of the Abbey, Leysdown gained her parochial freedom and complete parish rights.

From this same parish register we find the bounds of Leysdown Parish set out. --- The south side begins at Cable Gate leading to Harty, and is bounded by hew (Yew), Fleet to ye sea, and ends at Shell-ness. The East side begins at Shell-ness, as is bounded by the sea, and ends at the old Dluice in ye salts towards Warden.

The north side begins at ye Old Sluice, and is bounded by ye water course towards Warden, and ends at an Elm Tree in ye corner of Mustards meadow wch parts it from Warden and Eastchurch; then it is bounded to ye west, and runs across ye said meadow to an Elm in ye 8 acre hedge, and so on across ye 8 acre to an Elm in ye hedge next to Danes; then it is bounded to the north by ye fence, and ends at ye Elm tree at ye corner of ye Vicarage Glebe, next to ye 50 acres of Rayham Farm in Eastchurch.

The west side begins at an Elm tree in ye corner of ye Glebe aforesaid and is bounded towards Eastchurch by ye fence yt parts ye Glebe, and 50 acres to ye west, and runs strait to a tree in ye bottom of ye fence yt parts ye 50 acres of Rayham and ye 9 acres of Little Rides; then it is bounded to ye north by ye fence at ye bottom of ye said 50 acres, and runs about 30 rods to another tree in ye same fence; then it is bounded to ye west and runs strait across ye 25 acres and 30 acres fields of Little Rides Farm to a post next to Little Cable Hill, abt 10 rods from ye corner of ye said hill; and then runs catering to a post on ye brow between Great Cable and Little Cable Hill, and then it is bounded by ye fence between ye said hills, and ends at Cable Gate leading to Harty.

This is a true account of ye bounds of Leysdown Parish, according to a survey thereof made, May 22. 1734, by us --- John Woodroofe, Vicar; John Swift, overseer; John Sols ...?, carpenter of Eastchurch for 40 years.

Leysdown School

School at Leysdown was first held in a private house.

These Dames schools were closed by Forster's Act of 1870.

On January 13th 1871, a vestry meeting was held for the purpose of considering the Elementary Education Act of 1870, and Captain Hilton, Lord of the Manor, offered premises for the use as a school and residence for the headmistress at a rent of £100 per year. The first log-book that can be traced, is dated Nov 18th 1877. An entry states -- This school which has been closed over three months, was re-opened today. The children are noisy and disorderly, and if they ever did know anything have forgotten it. Children present 29. Signed M.M. Maguire.

Miss Maguire was evidently a lady of decided views, for we learn that on December 2nd a change has come over the scene.

Order reigns and Mrs Tanner expresses herself pleased at the order of the school.

We next read--Many children suffering from ague this week;- Miss Maguire and the ague evidently had a subduing effect upon the scholars.

The school was under Church officers and managers.

Nothing was received from the State towards the building, nor any grant from the Diocesan Societies, nor any rent for the use of it. The Leysdown and Shellness Land Co gave the building, and the people of Leysdown made certain improvements.

At the quarterly meeting of the managers of Leysdown school held on July 9th 1888, the subject of school fees was discussed and it was decided that the original arrangements of fees, viz;- 4d,3d,2d,1d should be apportioned as follows;- For children whose parents are above the position of farm labourer 4d, in standards V,VI,VIII, 3d for each child in Standards below V.

For children of farm labourers in any Standard, 3d for one child, 2d for a second, 1d for each third and fourth. In the case of more than four children of one family attending the school, no fee to be paid for any child beyond that number.

In 1891 the fees were abolished. This continued until the new Education Act of 1919, when children over 10 years must attend a secondary school. After a number of years the school was closed, the pupils travelling to Eastchurch or Sheerness for their education. In the census of 1891, the population of Leysdown was 218. The school holidays began with harvesting and the children were paid to work in the fields and for bird-scaring.

In the year 1767, a young man named David Martin came to Leysdown as Curate and was later appointed Vicar. He died in 1821, aged 76 years, he was also the Curate of Eastchurch and is buried in a tomb beneath the Altar table in the church.

He evidently held socialistic views most advanced for his time, for he assigned a yearly charge of £6-8s-0 to some persons unknown, thereby binding the future vicars of Leysdown to an annual payment on the Glebe (6 acres) of the sum stated.

The payment was called Redeemed Land Tax. He realised the dream of present day socialism by taxing the land to its full value, but in this case the State does not benefit, for this tax has become the property of some private person.

Some of the entries in the register and Churchwarden's books of that time, may be of interest.

In 1767 the Church rate was 6d in the £ and amounted to £18-14-2 rateable value £1,490, the Curate, David Martin, received £1-10s-0 of the amount, the Clerk, £3-2s-0, including the price of two mops.

Seventeen hedgehogs account for six shillings and eightpence, 2d for a stoat and 4d for sparrows, mowing the churchyard cost 2/-. Nothing extravagant appears until we come to the interesting item of 18/11;- Chusing Officers, this weighty matter evidently entailed much talk and subsequent thirst, which was at the expense of the ratepayers. There appears to have been one person, Monk by name, in receipt of relief - a liberal dole of 5/3 was given. More to Monk, is the form of entry.

A Doctor Shove was paid £1-3s-0.

The sum of £1-13s-0 paid for work on the road, seems strange, the explanation is at hand; the farmers had a happy way of paying their rates by doing work for the parish termed Duty.

Not a fraction did they pay in coin; it was all Duty done.

The Church rate was paid in hard cash, hence its unpopularity.

In 1898, on Monday December 20th, a meeting was held by the promoters of the Sheppey Light Railway, to propose a railway line from Queenborough to Leysdown, it was carried unanimously.

In November of that year, terrible gales and floods did enormous damage to livestock and buildings.

From a Directory for 1901, we find the following information; land area 2,177 acres, water 2 acres, tidal water 195, foreshore 2033. Rateable value £1,104. Population (1891 census) 218, the chief crops, corn, canary and other seeds. Soil, heavy clay subsoil, clay and gravel.

The Hilton Trustees are the principal land owners and Lords of the Manor. From the same Directory we see; school accommodation 54, on books 50, average attendance 46.

The Inventory of roads, dwelling houses, shops etc;

Road to Mustards..Poor house; 4 cottages.

South side down road; New House Farm, (Mr Till) 5 cottages, 1 cottage, Paradise Farm, (MrKingsland), Church, Vicarage, (disused).

On road to Mustards..Little Brooks, Frog's Island, 1 cottage, Mustards Farm, (Mr Beal).

In Leysdown village..Little Groves Farm, on opposite side, Vanity Farm, Rose and Crown, shop, The Sisters Cottage, 4 Nutts Farm cottages, School House, School, 2 Black Houses, Mussel Cottage,Mussel House (Mr Hilton), Coastguard Station and cottages, Shellness Coastguard Station and cottages.

Before we move into modern times, let us present a general view of agriculture in Leysdown as in the whole of the Island also, taken from a government survey in the year 1794 (George III).

The roads were described as being good all the year round, owing to the plenty of gravel pits and beach. Four fifths of the island is grass land, with a liberal share of rich and good fattening land, but a great part is poor breeding land.

Most of the arable was considered exceedingly fertile in wheat and beans, especially towards the north of the island, Minster, Eastchurch and Leysdown. It was not well wooded as supposed for it is remarked;- There is hardly any coppice throughout the whole of the Island; there are some small furze grounds and bushy shaws on the hill, which afford shelter for hares and a few partridges and pheasants.

Good fresh water is very scarce; between Eastchurch and Minster there are few springs. In dealing with the nature of the soil, we are told:- The whole of the Island is a deep, strong, stiff clay; some parts are so very sticky in the Winter time that the plough wheels get loaded with dirt in one mass, so as to form the shape of a grind stone, and are often overturned with the great weight, on which account foot ploughs are sometimes used. The horses' shoes are frequently torn off.

The general method of cultivation was to grow wheat and beans alternately, on the gravelly parts, a few oats and barley were sown, but in small quantities. A few turnips were sown but of little use to the grazier on account of the land being too wet for folding.

Much clover was sown with great success. The land was ploughed in the Winter for beans using four horses which ploughed with great difficulty about an acre a day. The beans were drilled in Spring about 20 inches apart, as early as possible, and were horse hoed twice and were hoed and weeded by hand once.

After beans, the land was ploughed for wheat, in flat ridges with open furrows to carry away the water in Winter. The best wheat was generally sent to the London market, and frequently weighed 64lbs per bushel, and was of fine colour. It is worthy of note that the half rod system of ploughing for wheat was evidently the prevailing custom.

The upland pasture was wholly employed in breeding lambs, or feeding young stock; Lambs were sent out of the Island for the Winter to be kept by farmers, on turnips, and returned about the middle of April, at the usual charge of 2/6 per score; when they returned they were placed on the poorest of grassland for the Summer; the wether tegs remained as lean sheep another year.

They not being fattened until they were all three years old.

The sheep were sold at Smithfield by salesmen, whose commission, together with the expenses of droving, turnpikes etc: amounted to above elevenpence per head from King's Ferry.

This is interesting, as it shows that the fat sheep after being ferried over the Swale, were put into the hands of drovers, and by them driven by road to London.

The sheep were of the Romney Marsh breed, but the soil being much inferior to that in RomneyMarsh the sheep were smaller; fat wethers at three years weighed from 20lbs to 24lbs per quarter. The cattle were almost wholly of the Welsh sort, bought by farmers from drovers from Carnarvon, Denbighshire, and Anglesea. The calves grew fat on the coarse Sheppey grass and were usually sold to the butchers in June or July, and weighed from 22 to 26 score.

The horses bred for the plough were from a sort that had been in the Island time out of mind, and are described as being somewhat smaller than those of other parts of Kent. No mention is made of farm work being performed by oxen.

There were two sorts of ploughs used. The Kentish turn-wrest of a large size, with a long tow, which cost, complete with tackle £6. The other was a foot plough, which was often used in Winter owing to the stickiness of the soil. These cost 25/- each.

Wagons were made to contain one and a half chaldrons, and cost £27. Carts were made in two sizes, 30 bushels costing £7, and 20 bushels costing about £5-10-0. The drill was little used at seed time, being a new invention and much distrusted. The old method of hand sowing continued to be used. The average prices paid for labour in Sheppey, in the year 1794 were as follows, and they were considered higher than those paid in any other part of Kent.

Day labour per day - 2/-. Carpenter and 3d allowance, 2/6; Spreading dung per 100 cartloads - 3/- to 4/6. Threshing wheat per quarter - 2/6. Threshing oats per quarter - 1/-. Threshing beans per quarter - 1/-. Hoeing beans per acre, 3/6 to 5/-. Hoeing turnips per acre - 7/-. Making hedges per rod, 3d. Cleaning marsh ditches per rod 1/- to 1/3. Cutting ant hills together per acre, 10/- to 12/-. Reaping wheat per acre, 6/- to 12/-. Reaping beans per acre, 7/- to 10/-. Mowing oats per acre, 2/- to 2/6. Mowing clover per acre, 1/8 to 2/6. Mowing grass per acre, 2/6 to 3/6.

Waggoners wages for the year, board and lodging etc; 10 to 13 gns.

Second ploughman - 9 yo 20 gns. Third ploughman, 8 to 9 gns. Waggoners mate, 8 to 10 gns. Second boy, - 4 to 7 gns. Third boy, - 4 to 4 gns. Bayliff, 11 to 12 gns. Dairy maid, - 4 to 5 gns. Cook, - 3 to 4 gns. Women per day, 10d to 1/-. Girls per day, 6d to 1/-. Boys per day 6d.

Prevailing prices of food, as follows-

Beef per lb. 5d.	Ducks and fowls per couple. 2/- to 3/-
Mutton per lb. 5d.	Turkeys each 4/- to 5/-
Pork per lb 5 1/2d.	Geese each 3/- to 4/-
Veal per lb 6d.	Fat pig 1 month old each 3/- to 4/-
Best Cheshire cheese 6 3/4d per lb.	Potatoes per sack 4/- to 5/-.
Apples per sack 7/- to 8/-.	Rough meal per bushel 6/-.

In connection with labour, a law was in operation and enforced with much severity. It forbade a farm servant seeking employment outside his own parish; if he strayed looking for work in another parish it was the duty of the Overseer to make him return.

Rents were mostly £1 per acre. Leases of 21 years were usually granted. Farms were in great demand, and there was much competition for the best farms.

The Rectorial tithe was usually paid in kind, and the Vicarial compounded for. About this time there were some disagreements respecting the Vicarial tithes. It was settled by the farmers paying 2/- per £ on their rents plus a certain amount per acre on the various pasturage etc: which they cultivated; a great deal of grumbling and discontent was universal over this vexed question of tithes.

In the manuring of the soil various methods were used, cockle shells were laid thirty loads to the acre. Seaweed was also used.

Chalk was brought from the banks of the Medway, and town dung from Sheerness was also used.

It was at this time under Mr Gilbert's Act of Parliament, that discussion took place between all the parishes in the Island regarding the building of a House of Industry or Workhouse, for the benefit of the poor in Sheppey.

We leave the agrarian scene of former years and return to the early days of the 20th century. In a document dated May 1909, we read these history making lines:- The Aero Club are building sheds and preparing trial grounds for their club at Leysdown.

Work for local men is one of the good results of the advent of the Aero Club. New houses are to be erected, and a general movement in a forward direction seems to be the order of the day.

Long may Leysdown flourish.

During the month Messrs Short have begun to move their works from Leysdown to Stone Pitts Farm, which they have bought, and as their establishment there is likely to be permanent, we may expect to see some more houses built for the accommodation of their workmen. We have to congratulate the Hon: C.S. Rolls on his successful flight from Leysdown to Stone Pitts on Saturday November 20th 1909, which was witnessed by an enthusiastic group of spectators.

Thus; in the small hamlet of Leysdown was history made, and the birth of aviation took place. It was in this year that London journalists discovered Sheppey and Leysdown, and we are pleased to note that they said the roads are good, even in Sheppey, but the word even rather rankles in one's mind. This Island is rich in beautiful place names which have a meaning and a history. May we point out that the strategic importance of Sheppey was discovered by Charles I, and it has been a place of note for centuries.

We mention this well known fact to prove how very much behind the times the London journalists really are in thinking that they have discovered a primitive race in an unknown place.

In May 1910 at the coronation of His Majesty King George V, celebrations went on all day at Leysdown. School children paraded to church, and dinner for all the inhabitants was taken under the Vicarage trees.

The children then marched to Priory fields where sports were held and tea was given until nightfall. A grand display of life saving was given by H.M. coastguards. Tea was provided at the Rose and Crown for everyone.

The old people were not forgotten, each was provided with a bit of meat, about 4 lbs, and other comforts. The day closed with the lighting of the bonfire which burned with a brilliancy far beyond our expectations. It was a crowded day of glorious life and talked about for many a day afterwards.

In the year 1911 we read of the passing of the carrier, a few words of regret may be fittingly offered to the memory of the carrier. We live in times of rapid change, old customs and old ways are set aside, new ideas and a general desire to be up-to-date possesses the mind of the people. We did think the carrier as an institution was as stable as the constitution itself. We must adapt ourselves to the altered conditions of our social life.

Summer hats and garments can no longer be left to the tasteful selection of the carrier, tin-tacks, and hair-pins will in future involve a journey to Sheerness. For the carrier is no more.

In the census taken in 1911, the population figures of Leysdown numbered 151.

On August 1st, 1914, the first World War was declared, and on August 7th we read that the scouts of Leysdown were kept busy manning the signalling posts, acting as messengers and patrolling the telephone wires at night. Their services were invaluable.

On Christmas Day 1915, enemy aircraft passed over the church as carols were being sung. Mr and Mrs Ward of the Rose and Crown organised a fund for providing plum puddings and tobacco for the soldiers who were stationed at Leysdown and are now at the front.

Over £8 was collected as the proceeds of a concert.

At Easter of that year, Mr Love's water cart was supplying the drinking water for the district, and farmers were appealing for help in getting the crops in.

In 1917 the Rose and Crown was closed for a period awaiting supplies of beer. The old elm tree in the churchyard was blown down, and Mr Beal with his tratcor skillfully raised the fallen giant, and a new lease of life was given to it.

The K.E.C. issued instructions to teachers in case of air raids.

An appeal went out from the inhabitants of Leysdown to their more fortunate neighbours living in the town:- Dwellers in towns respectfully requested by their rural brethen to burn gas or electric light for illuminating and cooking purposes, thus leaving a supply of oil for their less fortunate brethen.

The War Agricultral Committee assigned 200lbs of sugar for jam making in Leysdown and Harty. The ladies were highly indignant as 265lbs of sugar was the minimum amount required for this purpose.

In 1918 Leysdown celebrated "Peace Day" in fine style. Traps and beflagged wagons were requisitioned and a happy crowd journeyed to the scene of action. A high tea was spread under the trees, the children walked in procession from the school, with flags and jazz instruments of torturous sound.

After tea, races and games were held until the time came for fireworks and the lighting of the bonfire, each child was given a souvenier of a china beaker. The good will and friendly gathering, made peace day a delightful memory.

The census taken in 1921 registered 221 inhabitants.

In 1923 Leysdown was becoming a popular holiday place. The Sheppey light railway transported hundreds of holiday makers. Forward looking London businessmen bought up acres of land and erected tents for the Summer season. It was suggested in all seriousness that the village be renamed Leysdown-Super-Mare. Complaints were being made by the residents about the litter resulting from these invasions.

The old coastguard cottages at Warden Bay were converted into a hotel and country club, the Manor was demolished and the ancient fireplace was rebuilt in the hotel, a vast holiday camp replaced the broad acres of wheat in Priory Field, Little Groves, and Vanity farms both shared the same fate, the ancient Nutts Manor was also pulled down and turned into a camping site. From these small beginnings Leysdown has grown to be a holiday town, caravans replaced the tents, and were replaced in turn by chalets.

During the second world war the Royal Air Force was stationed at Leysdown. After the war the building of holiday camps was accelerated. Owing to the increase of motor cars and the popularity of coach travel the Sheppey Light Railway became uneconomic to run and it was closed down in 1948-9. The pleasant country lane named Station Road was renamed The Parade, and clubs, fun fairs, amusement arcades, cafes and shops line the street.

In the 1955 Directory 120 modern dwellings were listed.

Leysdown continues to grow. Almost all the agricultural land has been built on. An act was passed to curb the spread of urbanazition preserving the countryside from Bay View to Eastchurch as agricultural land, thus retaining in some measure the original aspect of the rural area of Sheppey.

8 THE HISTORY OF HARTY

Harty is mentioned in the Domesday Rolls; as Heortege or Heordtu meaning the Island filled with cattle, and the dues of the Archbishop received at Easter from priests and churches were recorded as follows:- From Heortege 7d: the King holds of Herte 1 yoke: Osbert Paisfoire holds 1 yoke and 1/2 yoke in Hertege.

In the reign of Edward I (1229-1307) Harty was an island seperate from Sheppey, connected by a bridge called Tremseth Bridge. This was broken down by a violent inundation of the sea, and the channel made so deep that a new bridge could not be laid nor the old one repaired, and therefore the inhabitants maintained two ferry boats instead. They had always been responsible for the repair of the bridge.

In 1760 Capel Fleet had become so narrow and silted up, that Harty was an island only at high tide. It appears that at this period it was entirely pastureland, on which 4,000 sheep were feeding constantly; there was no village, and only six Lookers cottages, these people, twenty in number, being the only inhabitants. There was of course the Church and Harty Ferry Inn. The value of Harty in the King's books in the year 1760 is set forth as £20-6s-0 1/2, the yearly tithes being £2-0-7 1/2.

The Manor of Sayes Court, originally belonging to Odo, Bishop of Bayeux. After his disgrace it was given by William of Normandy to John de Fiennes.

During the reign of King Henry III. (1216-72) it belonged to the Champion family. Referring to this family, from an old document dealing with the assessments made to knight the Black Prince, we find the following:- the Lady de Champaygne, whose tenant was Bartholomeus Cryel, was rated on certain lands in Harty, by estimation 400 acres of salt and fresh marsh, parcel of the Manor of Westwood, and called Longhouse.

This land was known later as 'Bartholomew's' after the tenant.

The same Lady was also rated for the Manor of Sayes Court, formerly called the "Manor of Hartye - cum Norton and Newenham".

Later it passed into the Sayes family and in the years 1558-1603, Sir Thomas Cheyney was the owner. His son Lord Henry Cheyney exchanged it for other property.

The site adjoins the Church, but not a stone of it is left, the moat, however, is preserved almost its entire length and on the large circular mound within, the fortified manor must have stood.

Another important property in Harty belonging to the Champion family in 1216 was 'The Mote', now known as Park Farm. In the year 1561 it was sold for a fine under the description thus:-

A Manor or messuage, 60 acres of pasture, 20 acres of meadow, 60 acres of land, and 50 acres of marsh, the purchaser being Thomas Paramore. Later it passed into the possession of the Cheyney family.

An interesting event took place in connection with the purchasing of 'The Mote'. It was the last instance of a dispute being settled by combat between the litigants; Simon Lowe and John Keye were demandants against Thomas Paramore, disputing his ownership. The 'Writ of Right' was demanded, and the champions were chosen, being Henry Naylor and George Thorne; On June 18th 1571, before the Justices of Common Pleas and 4,000 spectators assembled at Tothill Fields Westminster, the two champions on horseback and fully accoutred appeared, ready to decide the ownership by a single combat.

When the cause was heard, however, the demandants were Non-suited and the champions discharged without coming to an engagement and Paramour retained the property.

The two men were asked if they would engage in a mock combat for the disappointed crowd, they replied that they had been asked to fight for justice, not to mention the mob, and refused.

The occasion is of interest because, arising from it, Thomas Paramour bacame something of a hero in Kentish eyes. He was buried in St Mary's Church in Thanet where there is a mural tablet to his memory with two curious verses; the first being Canterbury's acknowledgement of his worth as a Mayor, and the second verse Thanet's reply.

Without knowledge of the Tothill episode the lines have little meaning:-

Canterbury --- Thanks, Isle of Thanet for this champion
Of's never dying name, my chiefe glorie;
His trophie hath made me companion
Unto the proudest by his Victorie.

Thanet --- Indeed thy countrie and unpeopled plaine
Unworthy were his wit and employment,
And gladly do receive him home again
Resting contented with his monument.

Harty is a perpetual Curacy held with the Vicarage of Leysdown. It is the gift of the Archbishop of Canterbury three turns out of four. The Church of St. Thomas the Apostle dates from 1216. The oldest portion of the existing fabric is Norman work. The west wall is thicker than the other walls, the central Early English buttress must have been added or altered from its original character.

HARTY CHURCH, NEAR LEYSDOWN, ISLE OF SHEPPEY.   K.2020.

It would seem the present plan of the church (excepting the north chapel and the south chantry) is original, at that, the north aisle of the Nave without any 'lights', may have been secular buildings. So wrote Mr Clark, the architect to whom the work of restoring the church was entrusted in 1880, at a cost of £1,500.

If the original building was Norman, as seems probable for there are no traces of earlier work, then the church consisted only of a nave and chancel. The pointed arches on the north side and the round arches on the south side, have been plainly cut out of the walls at some later period.

This is evident from the fact that the lower part of a Norman window, now blocked up, is cut off by one of the pointed arches, and from the details of the work; consequently what is now called the north aisle, did not exist originally and some have supposed that it was built as a shelter for the pilgrims who used to visit the church in the reign of King Henry III. (1216). Again, the north doorway, which is now the only entrance to the church is clearly not the original principal entrance, being too narrow and inconveniently situated for such a purpose, while the doorway in the south wall, now blocked up seems as clearly to have been the original and possibly the only entrance.

There can be little doubt that in the now blank south wall there was at one time a window corresponding to that in the north wall, and it is to be regretted that this was overlooked when the church was being restored. In the 16th century considerable alterations were made, either by the Champion family, or by the Abbey of Faversham, by whom it was claimed the church was held.

Hasted, however, states that it was formerly possessed by the Benedictine Nunnery of Davington, to which it was given by Richard II in 1384, and which continued in possession until the reign of Henry VIII (1534). This was settled by Archbishop Hubert, who ruled that the Abbess had the greater claim.

The old pews supplanted the original oak benches; they were high, square, and generally uniform. On the back of one of them in the south side was cut the following inscription, which has been preserved:- These pews were built in the years of Our Lord 1682. Henry Martin, Churchwarden. The Rood Screen, with the entrance from the north chapel and the return 'parclose' parting off the north aisle, remain, and are rather unusually connected with wall panelling.

The chancel, as is sometimes found in work of the 13th century is at a lower level than the Nave, and this seems to have existed in the 15th or 16th century, as it is clear from the interesting dais to the side altar in the north chapel, which in all probability is original.

The roof of the church before restoration was open to the tiles and afforded an example of the mode of framing in the 15th or 16th century. The timbers were unusually wide apart, and had to be strengthened by intermediate rafters.

The framing of the bells, (now only one exists) is brought down to the floor of the church and supports a single 'bell-cot' with a capped roof.

The windows in the building are all of the Perpendicular style, except two in the chancel, which are Early English, and a small square headed 'light', which formerly was fitted with a casement of which the hooks remain, and was probably a 'lepers window', so called from the cicumstances that persons afflicted with leprosy were only permitted to stay outside the church during service time, the casement being then opened for them to hear and see what was going on, and so take part in the service.

These extracts from old Kentish wills show that the ordinary people in those days cared a great deal for their church:-

To the roofing of the church, 6/8. William Osborne 1464. (A.I.3.)
Harty, to the new making of the Rood Loft in the Church, three cows, Thomas Banny, 1467.
The fragment of brass in the floor is the remains of a brass to Elizabeth Howard 1610.

On the jamb of the north door is carved an ancient sundial, and an ancient iron alms-box on a wooden stand can still be seen near the door, and a very original church organ also.

Worthy of mention is the unique muniment chest, depicting a tilting match between two knights. A description of this chest was sent to J.R. Planche Esq: who was an authority on armour in 1873. From an old document I quote his reply:- I cannot quite make out the details of the armour. The helmet of the Victorious knight does not appear to me to correspond with that of his antagonist: but as far as I am able to judge I should be inclined to date the carving circa 1460. Not withstanding the appearance of the tilting helm alluded to, the general character of the costume and peculiarity of the saddles, with their sweeps or cuisses (example of which is to be seen in the Tower Armoury) are distinctly of the 15th century, and I should say somewhere abot the middle of it but it may be nearer the close ...

The Rev. Cannon Scott-Robinson, however, was of the opinion that the chest was of German work, or from the Low Countries, and that the date is earlier, perhaps at the end of the 14th century.

While studying Medieval art in Paris some years ago, I visited the 'Muse de Cluny' and saw a similar chest to that of Harty. It was larger, but the tilting knights were identical. I was informed that the 'Cluny' chest was 14th century and of Flanders origin, it was considered one of their rare treasures.

So we can say that the Harty chest is the only one of its kind in Kent, and probably unique in England.

In 1887, when a grave was being excavated, a large quantity of masonry consisting of rough stone and large flints weighing nearly a ton was unearthed, it seemed to be the remains of the original old churchyard cross. Many of these old crosses are still to be found in different parts of the country.

In 1879 an Early Bronze Age foundry was discovered in Harty, and the site of early Saxon earthworks or forts. The remains of the foundry are now housed in the Ashmolean Museum.

Harty Ferry Inn stands on the site of a much older building.

The ferry was in existance from time immemorial. It is not beyond reason to think that there might have been an inn on this spot in Roman times. As there was a Roman 'Look-out post' at Minster, and a Roman camp of some size at Faversham, the ferry at Harty would be the most likely place for servicing the small garrison on the Island, so what more likely place for a 'Bush house' and trading post than this spot.

In the 12th century, pilgrims visiting Harty Church from the Abbey of Faversham must have crossed over by the ferry and it is possible that the inn was used as a rest house in those days.

In later years Harty was a place of some importance when vessels bound for London and Rochester passed up the Swale, the East India Merchantmen called at the Ferry Inn outward or homeward bound with their precious cargo.

Sometime during the early 1950's, during alterations to the cellars, some tokens and a button of the East India Company were found, also an Elizabethan penny.

The inn had two stairways, one leading to the bedrooms used by seaman, it is said that the inn-keepers wife would wait at the bottom of the stairs so that none could escape payment.

The Ferry Inn is now a popular rendezvous for yachtsmen in the Swale, and a favourite haunt for holiday makers.

HARTY FERRY INN, NEAR LEYSDOWN, ISLE OF SHEPPEY. K.2022.

According to a directory for 1901. The parson lived at Parsonage Farm Eastchurch. The area of Harty was 2,642 acres of land, 345 of tidal water and 694 of foreshore, the assessable value £927.

The soil was clay, subsoil, clay and gravel, crops grown were corn and seeds (for seedsmen's use), good grazing, and oyster beds.

The school accomodation was for 50 pupils, there were 8 on the books. The dwellings were as follows:- Brewers Farm. Elliots School, School House, Church, Sayes Court, (Mr. A. Love) 14 cottages, Park Farm, Ferry House Inn, Mocketts, Long Farm and Telegraph.

In 1902 we read that 120 guests attended the annual coursing on Mocketts Farm in March; they had a capital days sport, usual lunch provided at the Sheep House.

The school was closed in 1919. The ferry boat fell to pieces in the 1940's and has never been replaced, the old winch still stands on the 'hard' as a reminder of ancient history.

In the 1955 directory the following dwellings were listed in Harty, Mocketts Farm, Forge Cottage, Ferry House Inn, Park Farm, Sayers Court Cottage, Long Farm. Telegraph Cottage, White Lodge, Swaylings, Ferry Road, Elliots, Mocketts Cottage, The Bungalow Sayes Court.

The population figures are thus:-

in 1891 ... 125 persons, in 1911 ... 87 persons, 1921 ... 26 and in 1978 ... appx 21.

The tombs in Harty Churchyard are of the Randal family of Borstal Hall:- John Randal - 1712. Thomas Randal - 1766, they were somewhat dammaged by a bomb which fell close to the church during the last war, but have now been restored.

The Ferry Inn is a popular place for visitors, Harty itself is a quiet backwater, much visited by ornithologists and naturalists where birds and wild flowers abound in their natural surroundings in this abandoned corner of Sheppey.

9 THE HISTORY OF WARDEN

Warden - (Watch dune) Wardune - (The High Watch place)

The small hamlet of Warden has almost disappeared, for here the coast erosion is at its worst, and within 700 years, two churches have been claimed by the sea.

The historian Hasted wrote of Warden:- Warden lies the next parish northward from Eastchurch,being usually called Warne by the inhabitants and neighbourhood. The parish is situated on the northern side of the Island, which consists only of two houses, stands nearly in the centre of it, on high ground, having the Church adjoining to it, near which the lands are mostly arable.

In the south west part of it, next to Eastchurch, there is a great deal of broom and furze, and below that, in the vale, much good pasture. On the south-east part, next to Leysdown, there is a deep watery vale, of nearly a mile in width; a part of which is salt marsh, being overflowed at high water; across which is the high road from Warden to Leysdown.

From an old document of 1272 we learn these facts:- The paramount Manor of Milton claims over this parish, subordinate to which is the Manor of Warden, which in the reign of Edward I (1272-1307) was in the possession of the family of Savage of Bobbing. In the year 1288 Simon de Wardune was Lord of the Manor. In 1468 the Norton family from Milton Regis were in possession.

King Henry VII in 1485 gave the Manor to a favourite, one John de Savage, after the battle of Bosworth Field. The De Savages remained until 1509 when Henry VIII gave it to Sir Thomas Cheyne.

In 1759 it passed to James West, a descendant of Thomas, Lord de la War, who, in the reign of Henry VIII was a man of great note.

Again Hasted writes in 1798:- The Church which consists of one aisle and a chancel with a small turret at the West-end, is a poor, mean, plaistered building. It is dedicated to St James, and for many years was in a dilapidated state, in so much that there had not been any divine service performed in it, excepting on the induction of a Rector, for a long time, the parishioners usually resorting to the adjoining Church of Leysdown for that purpose; but it has some years since, put into some kind of repair, and made but hardly fit for divine service; though the whole building seems so decayed by length of time, that it cannot last many years ---.

In 1836 Mr. Delamark Banks Esq: caused the dilapidated aisle and chancel to be renovated, and erected a new tower, with the stone of the Old London Bridge, which was rebuilt in the year 1767, and taken down in 1832.

In a newspaper of 1868, the state of Warden Church was remarked upon. The Archbishop of Canterbury said, It would be desirable to move the Church and rebuild it inland, but nothing was done, and ruthless hands despoiled it with impunity, carrying pews and pulpit away for firewood. Locks, doors, and keeper were stolen, the bellrope also. In 1885 the bell, however, which had a very sweet tone was taken to the Abbey Church at Minster.

The commemorative tablet and one pew were saved and are now in the garden of Stonebridge House Warden.

In 1887 the Parish Church of Warden was no more. Its remains had disappeared into the sea.

This Church was part of the Ancient possessions of the Crown, and continued so till Henry III (1216-72) by his charter in his 9th year (1235) granted it to the Hospital of St Mary, commonly called the Maison Dieu, in Dover, and the brethren there, for ever, in free, pure, and perpetual alms, which gift was confirmed by Henry VI (1422-61). In his second year, by his Charter of Inspeximus; before which this hospital was possessed of a Manor and lands in this Parish, by the benefaction of Simon de Wardune, who had given to it his whole mesuage and park adjoining to it, and one hundred acres of land in the field of Wardune, with the homage, suits, and services due to him from several persons, as mentioned by his deed of it.

Which gift was confirmed by Henry III in his 12th year (1228), and afterwards by henry VI in his 2nd year (1424) when he confirmed likewise this Church to it, by his charter of Inspeximus ---

The Church remained with the hospital until the dissolution in 1539, when it was surrendered, with all its possessions into the King's hands. After which this church was granted to Sir Thomas Cheyne, whose son, Henry, Lord Cheyne, in the reign of Queen Elizabeth exchanged it for other lands. Thus once again it came into the possession of the Crown.

The Queen soon granted to Sir Thomas Hoby of Bisham, whose son,

Sir Peregrine Hoby Esq: was possessed of it in the latter end of the reign of Charles I.

The Church of Warden is a discharged living in the King's Book of the clear yearly certified value of forty five pounds, the yearly tenths of it being nine shillings and sixpence farthing, which were formerly paid to the Crown Receiver.

Patrons and Rectors of Warden Church -----

Patrons.	Rectors.
	James Barnard 1595.
	O.B.T.1617.
Peregrine Hoby	Ofmund Cluiting.A.B
Gent:	Oct: 1617.
	John .... edes May. 1640.
The King, by lapse.	John Tudor clerk 1674.+
	O.B.T. 1689.
Godfrey Meynel Esq:	Robert Eaton clerk. 1689.+
	O.B.T. 1702.
The Archbishop.	John Cumberland A.B.1703.
	O.B.T. 1731.
Joseph Adshead.	William Owens 1731.+
John Sackfield	O.B.T. 1732.
John Burdus, Gent:	John Featherstone 1732.
Diana, widow of Fr.Hosier Esq.	John Woodruff A.M. 1734.
	Gilbert Allenson. A.B. 1735.
The King, by lapse.	John Kirby. 1776.
	John Rice. 1783.

Note, all these +++ were likewise Vicars of Leysdown.

Warden Manor has been occupied continually since it was rebuilt in 1468. It was first mentioned in the year 1219, when Sir John de Savage of Bobbing was in possession.

War damage revealed some original wattle walls of a house much earlier than that of 1219. A Priest's Hole inside the chimney, dating back to the Reformation, and an old fireplace and stone staircase came to light at this time. The walls of this particular room are about 2 1/2 ft thick.

Simone de Wardune held it in 1288, after that, Sir John Hobey.

In 1468 the younger son of the Norton family from Milton Regis was in residence. At this period of its history the manor was rebuilt and the arms of the Norton family placed over the old fireplace.

During the Wars of the Roses, it was a meeting place of the Yorkists, Henry VII confiscated it and gave it to Sir John de Savage, after the battle of Bosworth Field in 1485.

The De Savages held the Manor until the reign of Henry VIII. The King then gave it to Sir Thomas Cheyne. At this time it consisted of about two hundred acres and was called Warden Court.

The Manor in later years was again restored by Sir Geoffrey Mayville. After that, it passed into the hands of Admiral Hozier.

In the year 1790 Sir John Sawbridge was the owner. This worthy gentleman, as well as being Lord of the Manor, and a Magistrate, was a famous smuggler, in league with the gang which operated from the Royal Oak. A tale is told, that Sawbridge was at the Oak one night supervising the unloading of an illicit cargo, when his servant rode post-haste to inform him that H.M.Excise Officers were on their way to visit the Manor. Sir John mounted his horse and galloped madly through the woods, entering the house by the kitchen door. With only minutes to spare, he donned his nightcap and leapt into bed still wearing his boots and spurs.

When the thundering knock came, his servant opened the door and took the officers to his master, who berated his victors indignantly for disturbing his slumbers. The ghost of Sir John is said to haunt the Manor, and on the night of December 18th he is said to be seen in the form of a horseman galloping madly along the bridle paths from the Royal Oak.

Sir Edward Banks owned the Manor in 1831. He was the architect who designed Bank's Town, The Crescent, and the mansion which is now the Royal Hotel in Sheerness.

After Sir Edward Banks, Lord Higgs came into possession. During the 1914-18 war, the Manor was used as a small hospital.

In 1930 it was owned by the trustees of the late Mrs. Phyllis Jackson Cole. In memory of her, it became a holiday centre for the members of Toc. H. At this time, when alterations were being made, two pennies dated 1789 were discovered in a secret passage, a Roman key was dug up by the gatepost, and a clay church-wardens pipe was found in a wig cupboard which was revealed when a wall was demolished. The cupboard still contained the mushroom shaped wooden pegs on which the wigs were hung. A coaching horn was discovered in a room once used for the horses harnesses.

Warden Manor was used as a barracks during Oliver Cromwell's time, and remained so until the Restoration.

The weather vane is unusual, it depicts Sir Robert de Shurland and his castle at one end and at the opposite end sits the witch of Scrapsgate who foretold his death.

The ancient name of Warden Manor was restored after Toc.H. took over. It is now on the list of National Trust houses and is opened to the public for two days in the year. Owing to financial difficulties it can no longer function as a hostel for Toc.H. and its future is uncertain.

In the early 1900's there was a small inn at Warden called The Smack Aground. It stood where the post office is now, with the old cottages adjoining.

The population of Warden in 1901 was 30 inhabitants, in 1911, it was 17, and in 1921 the number was 23.

There are now several holiday camps at Warden, and in the Summer the gardens of the ancient Wheatsheaf inn and the country lanes are thronged with holiday-makers and visitors, who enjoy the unspoilt beauty of this small hamlet in Sheppey.

10 THE HISTORY OF ELMLEY

Elmele = The Elm Meadow

Elmley is mentioned early in Sheppey's history. In a list of fines dated 1197, Sharden of the Manor of Elmley is recorded with Stapendun of Sheppey.

The greater part of the Island in these days was in the possession of the family of Peyforer. Fulke Peyforer died in 1276 and left it to one, Pontyn, in the reign of Richard II (1377 - 99). It was possessed by Nicholas Pontyn, whose daughter, Julianna, conveyed it by marriage to Thomas St Leger. Joan, his heir, married Henry Aucher, and afterwards Robert Capys. It now came into the possession of William Cromer who already had a large estate there which had originally belonged to the Cobham family.

It was sold to Sir Walter Manny, whose only daughter, Anne, married John de Hastings, Earl of Pembroke. He died and his son John succeeded the title and estate, but he was unfortunatlely killed in a tournament in 1389, being then only seventeen years old.

The estate consisting of one thousand acres of land became the property of his heirs, Reginald Grey and Richard Talbot, who conveyed them in 1405 to Sir William Cromer whose son, William Cromer afterwards purchased the Manor of Elmley to add to the estate.

It continued in the Cromer family until 1613 when Sir James Cromer died leaving three daughters, one of whom married John, eldest son of Sir Edward Hales, and she on the partition of the estates entitled him to the possession of Elmley.

He died leaving a son, and in his descendants this manor remained until 1789, when Sir Edward Hales conveyed it to George Gibs Esq, of Harbledown, in whose family it was in 1828.

The church anciently belonged to the Priory of Leeds, but in 1448 it was granted by Henry VI to the Warden and Fellows of All Souls College Oxford.

In 1326, upon the 24th June, Archbishop Reynolds on account of the notorious inefficiency of Dunstan de Marisco, who had for eighteen years been Rector of Elmclc, commissioned one of his own chaplains to act as curator to the said Dunstan until the patrons of Elmele should appoint another rector to succeed him, this the patrons did in the following August and at the same time petitioned the Archbishop to assign a pension to the late rector out of the annual proceeds of the living.

Elmley is now a bird sanctuary and nature reserve and is one of the loneliest places in Kent but once it was a small flourishing parish with a cement works manufacturing Portland cement and until recently it was empty and abandoned.

In ancient days it was one of the Sheppey islands, for the Swale in that age presented a wide sheet of water comparatively smooth, at places it was said to have been five to seven miles in width, and between Harty and Elmley there opened a wide navigable creek which ran in, even at low tide, to the foot of the Sheppey hills.

Up to the time of the Normans this was the ordinary route taken by seafarers, later in history it was used continually until the port of Sandwich silted up. It was about this time that the Swale silted up also and the navigation of large ships became impossible.

Elmley is no longer an island, the waterway became a creek and a few years ago when the sea-wall was being strengthened, the creek itself was filled in.

Elmley was originally used for sheep feeding, then for agriculture. It has been the scene of several commercial or manufacturing failures, brick and tile making have been tried there and cement manufacturing, but all were unsuccessful.

In the year 1874, the ancient church was roofless and used as a cattle shed, Oxford University had a new one built but that too has gone. In the census of 1861, there were 35 houses and 140 inhabitants. In 1874, there were 42 houses and 140 inhabitants and in 1874 there were 42 houses and 204 inhabitants.

Under the Education Act of 1870, a school was deemed necessary. It was built beside the church in 1885 by the University, with accommodation for eighty pupils, the number on the books being forty-four. In an old document of 1887 we read that the annual school inspection took place on July 4th when "a very great improvement upon last year manifested itself". From this same source we learn that "Queen Victoria's Jubilee was kept in this loyal little island with all due ceremony, R. Wilks Esq." The Oxford University tenant of the farm gave all his work people and their families a substantial dinner.

The Rector and his wife, the Rev G.H. Mason and Mrs Mason provided tea for all the school children.

The Church, dedicated to St. James the Apostle, consisted of a plain nave and chancel, with an entrance porch in the south west. There was no tower or spire, but a bell turret containing one bell, plain glass windows and a floor of coloured tiles. The building was sheltered by a grove of elm trees, from which perhaps Elmley derived its name.

Services were held there every Sunday, but in 1934 when Igglesdon wrote about it, he states: "Services are held there about three times a year, one without fail the Sunday before St. James Day". Apparently a large congregation was not expected especially in the dark period of the year, for the lighting facilities of the nave consisted of six separate candles.

In the year 1891, the population had increased to 219 inhabitants and from a directory of 1901 there were 34 houses and 319 persons living there. A public house called The Globe Inn had been built, the people of Elmley used the ferry boat to the mainland for shopping excursions, the cost of which in 1934 was 3d return, the money going to Oxford University who owned the island.

In 1901 the area consisted of 1,956 acres of land, 17 acres of water, 440 of foreshore and 57 of tidal water, the assessable value being £1,063.

Elmley is four miles long and two miles wide, the soil is clay subsoil, clay and gravel, pastorage....corn, canary and rape seed were grown. The cement works closed down in 1902 and with the closing, Elmley was finished and the inhabitants left to seek work elsewhere. When the factory was demolished the houses were also and in 1919 the Kent Education Committee considered the closing of the "smallest school in England, that being Elmley, a detached part of the Isle of Sheppey, there being only five pupils on the books and three of them being the headmistress's."

The school was closed and the headmistress moved to Sittingbourne, the remaining children were taken by ferry each day to the school at Murston near Sittingbourne.

The church was closed and fell into decay, and that too like its predecessor was used as a cattle shed by the farmers who lived there. It was eventually demolished.

Elmley has figured in history, for when King James II planned to escape to France, disguised as a Mr Abbaday, he took refuge at Neats Court, the home of his friend, Sir Edward Hales. From there he rode with Sir Edward and his steward to Elmley on the night of December 11th 1668. There they waited in Kingshill Farm near Elmley church for the Hoy that was to take them to France.

The ship lay off Shellness to take in ballast. Unknown to the escapees the Faversham sailors had been warned of his possible escape and three boats in charge of William Amis set out to search for the King. The hoy was espied at about 11 o'clock at night. Captain Amis, being bribed by £50 had the travellers searched, as a result they were taken ashore about 10am the next day beyond Oare near Faversham at a place called The Stool. Sir Edward and his steward, Sheldon were carried ashore but the King, disguised as a Jesuit, was not recognised and was left to wade ashore and fend for himself.

Here they were met by Sir Thomas Jenner's coach and about twenty gentlemen from Faversham on horseback who took them to the Queen's Arms at Faversham (now No 12 Market Place) and Sir Richard Marsh who saw them alight from the coach, recognised the King and was astonished and said: "Gentlemen, you have taken the King a prisoner", which wrought great amazement among them all.

The King asked them to convey him away at night in the Custom boat and pressed upon them that if the Prince of Orange took away his life, his blood would be upon their hands. They refused, however, and said that they must be accountable to the Prince of Orange.

King James was then taken from the Queen's Arms to the Mayor's house. A strong guard of soldiers and sailors watched over him until 10 o'clock on Saturday December 15th. The King sent to the Lords of the Council to inform them that the mob had robbed him of money and necessaries and desired them to send new supplies to him.

They forthwith despatched the Earls of Faversham, Hillsborough, Middleton and Yarmouth with about 120 horseguards besides sumpter horses, padnags and coaches whose orders were to prevail with the King if possible to return to Whitehall, but not to put any restraint upon his person if his resolution continued to leave the Kingdom. The Lords reached Sittingbourne on Friday evening and the King joined them on Saturday morning. He slept that night at Rochester and journeyed on to Whitehall the next day.

After being taken to London, he made up his mind to leave the country and on December 18th set out by barge for Gravesend. He arrived at Rochester on the 19th. On the 23rd he left the house of Sir Richard Head and secretly boarded a pinnace accompanied only by his illegitimate son, the Duke of Berwick and a manservant. He made for Queenborough where a smack awaited him, thence he crossed to the Essex shore and set sail for France on December 24th, arriving on Christmas morning off Ambleteuse where he was taken ashore in a French frigate...never to set foot on English soil again.

Sir Edward Hales was detained in Maidstone jail, then tried and sent to the Tower where he remained for one and a half years, afterwards rejoining the King in France.

In 1965 some workmen were demolishing the old buildings at Elmley and found an old coin. Upon being cleaned it was seen to be a large penny piece of the reign of James II.

The Isle of Elmley was purchased from Oxford University and is now a wonderful nature reserve and bird sanctuary. Kingshill Farm is the home of the Warden, the old school is a storehouse and since the new ferry bridge was built and the old road diverted, Elmley is more than ever one of the lost villages of Kent.

11 THE HISTORY OF SHURLAND HALL. EASTCHURCH

In the Domesday Map it is called Scipe, in 1240 Scirland, in 1690, Shoreland

In the year AD 893, the Danish Prince Hoestan built a fort on this site. King Canute resided there in 1017.

The De Shurlands came with William of Normandy, and in the reign of King Henry I it was in the possession of Sir Jeffery De Shurland who was a great favourite of that King.

But it was his son, Sir Robert De Shurland, who gave the great notoriety to the name, whose monument, with the strange accompaniment of the horses's head, lies in the Abbey Church.

Alas, the house of Sir Robert De Shurland survives only in name. Not a vestige of the thirteenth century building remains; all has long since disappeared to make room for a house still bearing the old name, and almost more historic as the residence of the Cheyney family.

Sir Robert had no son to inherit. His only daughter Margaret married Sir William Cheyney of Patricksbourne and the Cheyneys became Lords of Shurland.

Sir Alexander, the father of Sir William Cheyney had been brothers-in-arms with Sir Robert De Shurland, and both had been dubbed Knights-Banneret by Edward I for gallantry at Carlaverok.

The Cheyney family had no mean record to show during the 14th and 15th centuries and early part of the 16th century.

Covering the period between the reigns of Edward III and Henry VIII, members of the family had represented the County of Kent in Parliament no less than ten times, while Shurland House had been the scene of at least eight Shrievalty banquets given by a Cheyney.

Sir Robert Cheyney, the son of Margaret De Shurland, was three times elected Knight for the Shire of Kent - in the years 1348, 1351 and 1357. His grandson Sir William represented the county in 1416 and the following year was appointed Justice by Henry V and Chief Justice of the King's Bench by Henry VI ten years after.

His son, Sir John, sat for the county in 1449 while his grandson, again a

Sir John has a still more prominent place in the history of his country. He not only sat for the county but was also Speaker of the House of Commons.

A staunch Lancastrian, he was made a Knight-Banneret by Henry VII for his gallant conduct at the Battle of Bosworth Field and two years after had the further honour of being made Knight of the Garter and created Baron Cheyney of Shurland.

As he left no son, the title became extinct for a time and the estates passed on his death in 1496 to his nephew Thomas, the son of his younger brother William. Under him the star of the House of Cheyney rose to its zenith and culminated in a visit of Royalty to Shurland House.

It was this Sir Thomas Cheyney whose costly monument lies in the Abbey Church.

Along its edge may still be traced the record of his posts of honour. Beginning his public life as a favourite of the then all-powerful Wolsey, he was, in 1520, admitted as one of the six gentlemen of the Privy Chamber, then a Privy Councillor, Treasurer of the Royal Household and a Knight of the Garter. He was also Warden of the Cinque Ports, Constable of Queenborough Castle and Lord Lieutenant for Kent.

It seemed not to matter who was on the throne, whether Henry or Edward, Mary or Elizabeth, he adapted himself to each and retained his offices in the Council and the Household under all.

He was, meantime, adding manor to manor, chiefly as gifts from his Royal Patron, such as the suppressed Priories of Faversham, Davington and Fordwich, the historical Castle and lands at Chilham, besides many other Kentish manors, holding withal the ancestral estate of Patricksbourne Cheyney.

In addition to these he owned the wealthy manor of Tuddington in Bedfordshire which came to him through his wife, the daughter of Sir William Broughton. These all helped to swell the Shurland rent roll and enabled him to entertain with fitting magnificence Henry VIII and the fair but frail Anne Boleyn in 1532.

Before this royal visit and possibly in anticipation of the honour, Shurland House was expanded out of materials of which he had despoiled the noble old castle of Chilham, until it became a worthy place for the reception of and resting place for the greatest of the Tudor monarchs in one of his progresses.

Then, apparently, a wing on either side spread out from the central gateway which, with its flanking towers and their new stairs, claims a somewhat earlier date.

Then came the banqueting hall on the east of the main court, the dormitories on either side, one court after another, till the whole range spread over several acres, comprising no less than nine quadrangles, enclosed within high stone walls with a Chapel in the far south east corner, the whole forming a worthy mansion for a man who was styled Strenus Miles.

This visit of Henry was probably prompted by the whim and the vanity of that beautiful siren Anne Boleyn, then in the heyday of her beauty and power, in her desire to see the one time abode of an ancestress of her own, for an aunt of hers had married a Cheyney.

It was a whim which her then infatuated adorer could not but gratify, and a loyal subject, the recipient of so many favours, could not but accept at whatever cost.

A Royal progress, however, in those days involved an expenditure which could hardly fail to draw deeply on the resources of even a wealthy noble and if Sir Thomas, if all the more proud, was all the poorer for the distinguished presence of Royalty, even for two days. It was doubtless a gorgeous spectacle which the Lord of Shurland Castle provided for the King in that truly baronial abode; but it was a shortlived glory that then floated over Shurland House.

Forty years after, this lordly mansion had sunk into a neglected, dilapidated, rarely tenanted country house. Like so many others, it is a sad tale to tell.

Sir Thomas lived to see Elizabeth ascend the throne and on his death in 1559, was succeeded by his son Sir Henry Cheyney, who had married the only daughter and heiress of the wealthy Lord Wentworth.

Sir Thomas had married the rich heiress of Tuddington in Bedfordshire, where he had a princely estate, but Shurland had still retained charms for him. Not so with Sir Henry. Not all that Kent could offer him was to be compared in his mind with Tuddington domain, so he resolved to make that his home and to make it eclipse Shurland House.

Here he erected what he described as a Noble Mansion and, not to be left behind by his father's visit of Royalty, succeded in attracting Elizabeth on two occasions (in 1563 and 1573) to honour him by including

Tuddington in her progresses.

In reward for his lavish hospitality, the Queen revived in his person the title which had lapsed on the death of his great-uncle Sir John, and attached to it the name of his estate, raising him to the Peerage as Lord Cheyney of Tuddington. But in his case it was a still more fatal honour; it involved a still more costly sacrifice; it added fuel to the reckless display in which he indulged to such an extent as to become known as The Extravagant Lord Cheyney. The result was easy to foresee - he lived a spendthrift and died little better than a beggar.

That pile which his father had accumulated and left to him was fast crumbling away; the estates which had made him one of the wealthiest of Kentish gentry were rapidly dispersed; manor after manor disappeared from his rent roll; even the beloved and vaunted Tuddington shared the general decay, and so utter had that decay become that Lysons says of it, "nothing but the kitchen remains".

Meanwhile, Shurland House felt the sad consequences of the change. Even to the ears of Elizabeth came up the bitter cry of a neglected tenantry. Where the grand old Knight Sir Thomas had kept in his house ordinarily eight score serving men besides retayners, gentlemen and others that were ready for all types of service, or danger of invasion, numbering at least 400 persons, by the year 1570, Shurland House was standing empty, farm-houses had fallen into decay, the island itself was well nigh depopulated, the land lay uncultivated and the defences of the coast were perilously exposed.

Such was the state of things when the Manor of Sheppey and Shurland House, which had for so many generations gone together, were separated - when the old ancestral home, of which Shurlands and Cheyneys had been so proud, by some process of exchange reverted to the Crown.

Queen Elizabeth at once saw the exposed and undefended condition of the island and, realizing the danger, set herself to restore, if it were possible, its prosperity, and to strengthen its fortifications.

She had heard that many towns in Flanders and France were maintaining a large population, as well as creating a remunative industry, by the manufacture of leather. Now the Isle of Sheppey still retained its fame as a producer of sheep. Its pelts or plucked wool, its sheepskins and lambskins she determined to turn into account; they should become a source of revenue and bring together by traffic with the Continent a seafaring population.

Already a Merchaunte Stranger, one Andreas or Andrew de Loo (or Delow as sometimes called) had obtained a licence for leather production in the neighbouring Isle of Grain. Why should not the licence be extended to Sheppey and a monopoly of restricted sale be established here?

This would soon bring together a class not only of manufacturers and traders, but a body of men who might be utilised for the Navy and the Forts, increasing the revenue by export dues, and convert the island from being as it then was, an element of weakness, into a source of strength - to transport, subject to payment of custom, not more than 4,000 sheep felts, 2,000 sheepskins and 4,000 lambskins. (In addition to its repute as a pasturing for sheep, it was famous for producing honey.)

What, you may ask, has this to do with the history of Shurland Hall? A great deal. In a lease granted by Elizabeth in 1580 is a stipulation that the tenant farmer shall convert ten of the outer chambers or rooms of the said house into tenements and new build on the premises five other tenements, and in them to place ten able men to serve with caliver, pike, bowe and such other like weapon for the defence of the island....and in the residue of the said house some honest and sufficient person with his family to dwell, and it shall be lawful for Her Majesty, if she please, to take down and sell certayne of the outer houses there, being superfluous.

Thus was Shurland House turned for a time into a barrack, and the last quoted clause explains how in the course of time the old mansion fell into its present condition.

Shurland Hall remained with the Crown until the beginning of the reign of James I, when in 1605 he conferred what is termed in the Grant the Capital Mansion of Shurland to his beloved and faithful servant Philip Herbert, Knight, the younger son of the Earl of Pembroke, whom he created Lord Herbert of Shurland and Earl of Montgomery. His elder brother William dying without sons, he succeeded to the family Earldom of Pembroke in 1630, was made Lord Chamberlain to Charles I in 1625 and Chancellor of the University of Oxford in 1641, and was the last to hold the office of Constable of Queenborough Castle.

He married as his second wife the famous Ann, Countess of Dorset, of whom the following anecdote is worth telling.

When Sir Joseph Williamson, the Secretary of State to Charles II, wrote to her naming a candidate whom he wished her to nominate for her pockct borough of Appleby in Westmorland, the Countess replied, "I have been bullied by an usurper; I have been neglected by a court; I will not be dictated to by a subject."

The History of Shurland began with the traditional enterprise of the dauntless Baron Sir Robert. It may appropriately close with the anecdote of the equally dauntless Countess.

The fall of the great house of Shurland continued. It was no longer the home of the Lords of Sheppey. It became over the years a gentleman's residence, then it was occupied by tenant farmers, in 1840 Robert Holford Esq was the owner. It passed from farmer to farmer and in 1908, Mr Till did much to restore the Hall and was recognised as the first farmer to go in for extensive agriculture.

SHURLAND HALL, EASTCHURCH, SHEPPEY ISLE

In the early part of the First World War, soldiers were garrisoned there and a great deal of damage was done. Fireplaces and panelling disappeared and gales continually ripped off roofs and walls, till finally the old hall was used to store farming implements and cattle fodder, the lead roofs were torn off by vandals and the destruction was complete.

Now, alas, nothing remains but the strong outer wall and the facade of the noble gate-house to remind us of this once great Hall.

In the 1930s, the wife of the then owner was discussing the haunting of Shurland and this is what she had to say. A ghostly lady dressed in black silk and a large black dog were sometimes seen. Bells would ring from some unknown cause, and the sound of horse's hoofs were heard outside the front door, and it was said that a hearse passed by. We would rush to the door and open it, but nothing was to be seen.

All bedroom doors were locked at night and any one of the dogs would whine if you tried to get him to pass into one of these rooms and absolutely refuse to enter. Door handles would keep turning and ghostly fingers would run over the panels of the door.

Huge hairy spiders infested the place, and it was always said that they foretold death. Outside at night the owls screeched and weird noises kept the inmates of the mansion awake. The lady of the house said, that she herself was not afraid, but it was very difficult to persuade her guests to stay.

CHRONICLE OF EVENTS IN SHEPPEY

A.D. 161	First mentioned by PTOLOLNMY, called TOLIAPUS.
664-675	MINSTER ABBEY built.... QUEEN SEXBURGA. first abbess.
669	SEXBURGA dies.
709	SEXBURGA canonised.
798	First Danish invasion.
832	Second Danish invasion.
855	Danes dominated Sheppey.
871	King Alfred fortified Castle Rough Milton.
893	Danes came to stay...Prince Hoestan built forts at Shurland (Scipe) and Queenborough.
1071	Canute stayed at Shurland. (Scipe)
1052	Earl Godwin attacked Sheppey....destroyed Minster Abbey.
1066	William the Norman installed Barons in Sheppey.
1130	Minster Abbey rebuilt and Parish Church added.
1131-1154	Minster flourished.
1248	Leysdown Church built.
1272	Harty Church built.
1279	First Eastchurch church built.
1363	Queenborough Church built.
1366	Queenborough Castle built by King Edward III.
1377-1399	King Richard II ordered coastal defences.
1406	King Henry IV ordered better roads....Levied tolls on ferry.
1431	Second Eastchurch built.
1448	Isle of Elmly granted to All Saints College Oxford.
1450	Jack Cade's rebellion...attempted to seize Queenborough Castle.
1464	George Plantagenet, Duke of Clarence, made Constable of Queenborough Castle.
1539	Dissolution of Minster Abbey...sold to Sir Thomas Cheyne.
1554	William Cromer of Borstal Hall imprisoned, estates given to Cheyne.

1558	Queen Elizabeth gives Cheyne more manors.
1559	Thomas Cheyne dies.
1560	Lord Henry Cheyne disposes all his estates including Shurland Hall.
1571	Sir Humphrey Gilbert purchases site of abbey, farm, and gatehouse.
1582	Queen Elizabeth fortifies Shurland becomes the Lady of the Manor.
1579	First chemical works started at Queenborough.
1594	Queen Elizabeth re-built Scocles and indentured it to Sir Edward Hoby for 31 years at an annual rent of 6/8.
1603	Lord Hudson, Lord of the Manor of Kingsborough, was sent to Scotland to notify King James IV of his succession to the throne.
1604	Sir Phillip Herbert was created Baron Herbert of Shurland, he was the last constable of Queenborough Castle.
1625	Queen Henrietta Maria, wife of Charles I received Neats Court as part of her wedding dower
1649	Sir Michael Livesay of Pasonage Farm, Eastchurch, signed the death warrant of King Charles I. with Agustine Garland, M.P. for Queenborough.
1660	Restoration of Charles II...Livesey murdered in Holland....Garland transport sold into slavery
1665	King Charles II. with Samuel Pepys plans Sheerness dockyard and garrison.
1667	The Dutch invade Sheppey.
1669	Royal Dockyard built and garrison fortified.
1688	King James II tried to escape to France from Elmley.
1732	William Hogarth and friends made a perambulation to Sheppey and stayed in Queenborough
1734	Leysdown church rebuilt....Rev. John Kershaw.
1745	Stephen Rouse came to Minster and kept a diary for forty years.
1786	First Wesleyn chapel built at Blue Town.
1787	Bethel Church built at Blue Town seating 800 people.

1788	Danely Farm rebuilt.
1790	Roman Catholic Church built at Mile Town seating 400 people.
1797	Richard Parker organised the Mutiny at The Nore, hanged June 15th.
1803	Napolonic scare...Moat dug for defence Sheppey Volunteers formed.
1806	Army reserve 70,000 "Army reserve for Home DEfence". Call up 18 to 45 years.
1812	Weslyn Chapel enlarged to seat one thousand Sunday schools started.
1813	Sunday School enlarged 330 girls and boys and 30 teachers. Baptist or Zion Chapel built in Mile Town seating 200.
1820	Admiralty House was built for William Duke of Clarence (The Sailor King) He was the the last Royal connection in Sheppey.
1825	Sir Edward Banks planned a select warering place laid out The Crescent, Banks Terrace, and built the Royal Hotel.
1828	Dockyard Church built.
1831	Sir Edward Banks carried out improvements to the Dockyard.
1832	Queenborough disenfranchised...end of the 'Rotten Borough.'
1832	Jewish Synagogue built in Sheppey Street Blue Town, Rabbi Cohen.
1834	Great cholera epidemic in Sheppey. Parish unions established, Parish guardian.
1836	Holy Trinity church built.
1837	Queen Victoria restored all Sheppey churches.
1860	First bridge and railway built.
1871	Population census of Sheppey 18,434.
1872	St. Paul's Church built.
1873	Minster School opened.
1874	Present Leysdown church built.
1880	Harty Church restored.

1883	Queenborough Charter...four Aldermen and 12 Councillors elected annually, now an important port. Ships sail twice daily to Flushing.
1885	Third Dockyard church built. Elmley School built....cement works opened.
1888	Local and District Councils formed, Rural, Urban, Queenborough.
1895	First Rural District council meeting, Rate 1/- in the pound.
1902-1904	Light railway to Leysdown opened, Electric trams in Sheerness.
1903	Waterworks dug at Minster...many relics of historical interest found.
1905	Mr. Ramuz of Minster, planned to make a museum in the gatehouse also to have the have the area excavated by Oxford University Arch. Society.
1911-1912	Eastchurch became the cradle of aviation.
1914	Aerodrome at Eastchurch...troops stationed at Shurland and all large houses.
1914	H.M.S. Bulwark blew up in Dockyard.
1914-1918	Army huts. Liberty Hall now Working Man's club.
1915	H.M.S. Irene blew up in Sheerness Dockyard.
1915	Leysdown starts a camping site, tents were rented at Nutts Farm, excursion trains ran direct from London for 2/6d return.
1917-1918	Land sales begun in 1904 now very popular, Many houses built.
1920	Minster Working Men's Club opened...Mr. Ramuz and Mr. A. Ingleton directors.
1920	Great development in camping facilities at Leysdown.
1929	The Nore Lightship ceased to be used by Trinity house.
1931	Ferry tolls abolished after 525 years.
1939	During second world war Sheppey became a closed area.
1940	Eastchurch aerodrome bombed, lives lost, Defence forts built in the Estuary and boom defence placed from Shoeburyness to Minster.

1948-1949	The Sheppey Light Railway was closed.
1949	Borstal Hall burnt down.
1950	Elmley Church demolished.
1953	A great flood did much damage to Sheerness, The sea wall was rebuilt.
1954-1955	The village of Westminster ended, inhabitants re-housed, buildings destroyed.
1960	The new Ferry Bridge opened by Princess Marina, Duchess of Kent.
1960	The Dockyard closed after 290 years.
1962	Elmly Church demolished. The Tombstones were removed to Eastchurch.
1968	450 coins were dug up at Clark's Farm whilst digging the foundations of the new school. They dated from Edward IV (1461 - 1483) and 1660-1685, sold at Southebys.
1969	Friendship House opened by Percy Mount Sept. 23rd.
1971	A train failed to stop at the station, demolishing it and killing one woman and injuring seven others.

The Technical School in the Broadway, Sheerness, which was built in 1910 and had educated many famous men, closed in 1971. The pupils were transfered to the new comprehensive school.

In 1972 the Steel Works in Bluetown was officially opened by the Duke of Edinburgh and has done much to solve the problem of unemployment. In 1973 Pilkinton's Glass Works closed and in the same year decimal currency was introduced.

In 1973 Pilkington Glass works closed.

In 1974 the Island Councils were incorporated into the Swale Borough Council. Sheppey no longer had a separate identity.

In January 1975 the Olau Line started a daily service to Flushing. It had developed considerably over the years and the docks were in business and expanding.

In 1976 the old Technical School was finally demolished and the Blackburn Home built on the site. There was a proposal for Shurland Hall to be restored by the Landmark Trust but unfortunatly this did not materialise. In this year, also, the village of Westminster was abandoned and a new road was built to Sheerness with the Sheppey Way.

In 1977 the Sheppey Local History Society persuaded the Swale Borough Council to lease the almost ruined Abbey Gatehouse to the Society. The members cleaned out pigeon droppings almost two feet deep and sold this guana to local gardeners for twenty pence a bag. This money started the Gatehouse Museum Fund. Several young men worked under the Youth Opportunity Scheme helped to make the Gatehouse habitable. The Local History Society members held Jumble Sales and other events to raise money for the restoration of the Gatehouse. A cellar, lined with Elizabethan bricks was dicovered. An old well was uncovered also. The Kent Archeological Rescue Unit came at several weekends, to advise and supervise the work. Old display cases were purchased from shops which were closing down to provide places to display museum artifacts and local artist. Harold Baxter, painted pictures of Sheppey's past, which were hung in the top room.

On New Year's Day 1978, Sheppey was cut off from the mainland for several days with snow and floods. The road-cleaning equipment was at Sittingbourne. Again, in January 1979, Sheppey suffered another flood.

The Maidstone and District Bus Office and Waiting Rooms were demolished in 1981 and the Abbey Gatehouse aquired two long seats from the demolished office.

On 2nd April, 1982, the Abbey Gatehouse was officially opened with a grand ceremony. This was an occasion of great excitement as many notable Island people were present with all the island vicars and the Mayor and Mayoress of Faversham. At the last minute, the Member of Parliament who was due to perform the opening ceremony, was unable to attend because of the Falkland Crisis. The Mayor of Faversham stepped in to perform the ceremony. This museum has proved very popular and over the years has aquired a professional aspect, being mentioned in all the Guide Books and Tourist information. Not long after it was opened, thieves broke in and stole four of the pictures of old Sheppey. The inhabitants of Minster were outraged and a firm installed a burglar alarm free of charge. These pictures were never recovered but Harold Baxter repainted the same scenes for the museum.

A bronze medallion depicting a scene in Brielle, Queenborough's Twinned Town, was presented to the History Society in 1982.

In 1983, the Queenborough houses where Hogarth and his friends stayed on their famous 'peregrinations', were in danger of being demolished. The Local History Society and others vigorously protested and an enquiry was held. This resulted in a preservation order being put on them. Later these houses were restored to their former glory.

An Open Prison was created on the site of the old aerodrome at Eastchurch and two more prisons have since been built in the same area, making a total of three prisons on Sheppey.

In 1986, there was a proposal to build a new Church Hall at Minster Abbey Church with a covered walkway between the church and the new hall. As this would involve knocking a hole in the wall of the old church, and building on the site of a Saxon Monastry, many people protested. An archaeological excavation was carried out. Foundations of the old monastry were discovered along with three graves. Afterwards, permission was given for a new church hall to be built of suitable material and the height was to be no greater than that of the church.

On 22nd October 1987, a hurricane devastated the south of England. The historic holm oak tree known as the Crusaders Tree, which grew in front of the Gatehouse, came crashing down. Part of the trunk now lies beneath the archway bearing a plaque on it and a giant acorn carved from its wood, lies on the windowsill of the top room in the museum. Keyrings, carved by a History Society member, from some of the remaining wood, in the shape of acorns, are sold in the Gatehouse shop and a new oak sapling planted by the Round Table on the site of the old oak.

In 1988 the old forge, dating from the 18th century, in Minster Village, was demolished and four houses built on the site. In the same year, Leysdown Church was demolished. This was the third church to be built on this site since 1216.

The United Glassworks closed in April 1990 with the loss of more than 300 jobs.

The Sheppey Comprehensive School was renamed the Minster College.

During 1992 documentary evidence was discovered which threw new light on the Robert de Shurland legend. It showed that Sir Robert died in France having lived there for the last three years of his life as Governor of a French city. His body was returned to England for burial in the family chapel.

The face of Sheppey has altered greatly over the last two decades. New roads have been built. Many new houses have been constructed. The sea walls have been heightened and the sea is no longer visible from the road in many places. Eastchurch and Leysdown are full of Holiday Camps. Minster has grown and is now a built up area. During the summer months Leysdown rings with the noise of a seaside town with Bingo, Fruit markets and traffic. There is no trace of the quiet, tree-lined lane going through the Spinney to the beach. Churches, once always open for visitors, are kept locked, although a rota of stewards open Minster Church and Gatehouse during the summer for the many people who come to see these old buildings. Fresh evidence of Minster's past has been discovered and preservation orders made for the site. Shurland Hall, once home of the famous Cheyne family, is now a derelict, empty shell with trees and bushes growing in what was once fine rooms.

Sheppey is still changing rapidly. As more houses cover the countryside more archaeological evidence reveals the mystery of the islands past confirming that Sheppey had an important place in England's history.

INDEX

162